THE TRUTH ABOUT
POSTMILLENNIALISM

THE TRUTH ABOUT POSTMILLENNIALISM

A Study Guide for
Individual or Group Bible Study

Kenneth L. Gentry, Jr., Th.D.

Chesnee, South Carolina 29323
"Proclaiming the kingdom of God and teaching those things which
concern the Lord Jesus Christ, with all confidence."
(Acts 28:31)

The Truth about Postmillennialism
A Study Guide for Individual or Group Bible Study

© Copyright 2019 by Gentry Family Trust udt April 2, 1999

All rights reserved. No part of this book may be reproduced in any form or by any means, except for brief quotations for the purpose of review, comment, or scholarship, without written permission from the publisher.

Unless otherwise noted, Scripture references are taken from the New American Standard Bible, © 1960, 1962, 1963, 1968, 1971, 1972, 1973, 1975, 1977, 1995 by The Lockman Foundation. Used by permission.

Published by:
Victorious Hope Publishing
P.O. Box 285
Chesnee, South Carolina 29323

Website: www.VictoriousHope.com

Printed in the United States of America

Cover design by Brian Godawa

Proof reader: Bill Boney

ISBN 978-0-9964525-7-1

Victorious Hope Publishing is committed to producing Christian educational materials for promoting the whole Bible for the whole of life. We are conservative, evangelical, and Reformed and are committed to the doctrinal formulation found in the Westminster Standards.

Dedicated to

Rev. Brad Sneed

Committed Christian, faithful pastor, good friend

TABLE OF CONTENTS

Preface 9
1. Introducing Postmillennialism 13
2. Postmillennialism in Creation and Covenant 25
3. Postmillennialism in the Psalms and Prophets 33
4. Postmillennialism in the Gospels 49
5. Postmillennialism in Paul 63
6. The Great Tribulation in Postmillennialism 75
7. The Book of Revelation in Postmillennialism 97
8. Interpretive Literalism in Postmillennialism 115
9. Israel in Postmillennialism 127
10. The Rebuilt Temple in Postmillennialism 137
11. Prophetic Time-frames in Postmillennialism 151
12. Objections to Postmillennialism 169
Conclusion 183
For Further Study 187

PREFACE

This is the second release in GoodBirth Ministries' *Truth About Series*™. This new book series deals with topics of deep significance and abiding interest to Bible-believing Christians. The studies are designed for serious Christians who love God's Word and want to better understand both it and the Christian worldview arising from it. The theme governing this series is: "Sanctifying God's People through God's Truth." Our undergirding theme verse is taken from Christ's prayer regarding his followers:

"Sanctify them in the truth; Your word is truth" (John 17:17)

The Point of the *About Truth* Series

The *Truth About Series*™ offers succinct, biblically-based, and carefully-structured studies specifically designed for either personal or small group Bible studies. Not only do the chapters breakdown the material in logical chunks, but at the end of each chapter we present two types of study questions:

- Review Questions that assist the reader in better comprehending the core issues dealt with in the chapter.
- Discussion Questions that promote further group reflection on the topic beyond that which is presented.

Unlike many Christian study guides the books in this series will deal seriously with the issues at hand, rather than skimming the surface, stating the obvious, or providing cute stories. The very issues studied merit due consideration because of their significance for the Christian worldview. We will assume the reader's deep interest in understanding the Bible and its relationship to the topic being analyzed.

The Significance of the *About Truth* Series

Our desire is to help remedy a problem that has plagued God's people from time immemorial and which is especially problematic today. God warned through Hosea: "My people are destroyed for lack of knowledge." In fact, he informed his Old Testament people that they went "into exile for their lack of knowledge" because their "honorable men" were "famished" and the multitude of the people were parched with thirst" (Isa 5:13). The writer of Hebrews chastises first-century Christians:

"You have become dull of hearing. For though by this time you ought to be teachers, you have need again for someone to teach you the elementary principles of the oracles of God, and you have come to need milk and not solid food. For everyone who partakes only of milk is not accustomed to the word of righteousness, for he is an infant. But solid food is for the mature, who because of practice have their senses trained to discern good and evil." (Heb 5:11–14)

Christianity is a revealed religion established on divinely-inspired truth claims. As the apostle Paul states: "For this reason we also constantly thank God that when you received the word of God which you heard from us, you accepted it not as the word of men, but for what it really is, the word of God" (1 Thess 2:13). Thus, we firmly believe that "all Scripture is inspired by God and profitable for teaching" (2 Tim 3:16; cp. 1 Cor 2:4).

God's word exercises a significant influence on the whole Christian life and experience. We become Christians through the instrumentality of his word: "for you have been born again not of seed which is perishable but imperishable, that is, through the living and enduring word of God" (1 Pet 1:23). Indeed, "faith comes from hearing, and hearing by the word of Christ" (Rom 10:17). Because of this Christians must "hold fast the word" unless they have "believed in vain" (1 Cor 15:2)

The role of God's word does not end with our new birth. Indeed, we are to grow and develop spiritually by means of that word: "like newborn babies, long for the pure milk of the word, so that by it you may grow in respect to salvation" (1 Pet 2:2). Paul speaks of Christ's love for the church in Ephesians 5:26 where he adds: "that He might sanctify her, having cleansed her by the washing of water with the word." Hence, Jesus' prayer to God in our behalf: "sanctify them in the truth; Your word is truth" (John 17:17). Therefore Christians must "let the word of Christ richly dwell within you" (Col 3:16) for "the word of truth" is "the power of God" (2 Cor 6:7).

God has given us the Scriptures "for teaching for reproof, for correction, for training in righteousness, so that the man of God may be adequate, equipped for every good work" (2 Tim 3:17). Therefore, the Christian must study and understand the Bible, for we are commanded to "be diligent to present yourself approved to God as a workman who does not need to be ashamed, accurately handling the word of truth" (2 Tim 2:15).

Then having learned God's word the child of God must apply it to his life, family, society, and culture. Paul insists that you must "speak the word of God without fear" (Php 1:14). He urges the believer to hold "fast the faithful word which is in accordance with the teaching, so that he will be able both to exhort in sound doctrine and to refute those who contradict" (Tit 1:9). As a committed Christian you are called to take "every thought captive to the obedience of Christ" (2 Cor 10:5).

From these several verses we can see the incredible significance of God's word on the Christian's life. Our *Truth About Series*™ is designed to minister to those Christians who are committed to understanding the Bible and the Christian worldview better.

Chapter 1
INTRODUCING POSTMILLENNIALISM

In this study we will be focusing on one of the great doctrines of Scripture: eschatology. The term "eschatology" is the compound of two Greek terms: *eschatos*, which means "last," and *logia*, which means "word, discourse." Therefore "eschatology" is "a study of the last things."

Theologians generally divide eschatology into two categories, personal eschatology and cosmic eschatology.

- *Personal eschatology* focuses on the destiny of the *individual* at death. It involves biblical teaching on physical death, the immortality of the soul, the intermediate state, heaven, and hell.
- *Cosmic eschatology* deals with the end of the *world*. It includes Scriptural teaching on the flow of history as it unfolds toward the end, concluding with the second coming of Christ, the resurrection of the dead, the final judgment, and the coming of the eternal state.

In our study we will focus on cosmic eschatology. Christian discussions regarding the end of history and the return of Christ are extremely popular today. Unfortunately though, the second advent is more deeply loved and firmly believed than biblically understood and accurately proclaimed. This is lamentable in that eschatology is a vital component of the Christian worldview. After all, eschatology deals with the God-ordained flow of history and the prophetically-determined end of the world.

The Significance of Eschatology

Before we actually begin considering eschatology per se, we must understand its significance for the Christian worldview. Let us reflect on three important observations:

The second coming exalts Christ's victory in redemption

When the Lord came to earth in the first-century, he came in a state of humility in order to suffer and die. Paul expresses this as follows: "being found in human form, he humbled himself by becoming obedient to the point of death, even death on a cross" (Phil 2:8; cp. Matt 1:21; Luke 19:10).

But Scripture does not leave him suffering on the cross or lying in the tomb. Rather, it presents his ultimate glorification in heaven through three steps: resurrection, ascension, and session (being seated at the right hand of God). Ultimately his mediatorial rule over temporal history will end at his *return* — to resurrect and judge all men and establish the final order. As Paul puts it: "God has highly exalted him and bestowed on him the name that is above every name, so that at the name of Jesus every knee should bow, in heaven and on earth and under the earth, and every tongue confess that Jesus Christ is Lord, to the glory of God the Father" (Phil 2:9–11).

Yet as Hebrews points out: "at present we do not yet see everything in subjection to him" (Heb 2:8b). So then, Christ's second coming is necessary for concluding his redemptive victory.

The second coming completes God's plan for history

In his first-century work, Christ conquers sin (Heb 10:11–14), death (2 Tim 1:10), and the devil (Heb 2:14). Yet all three evils remain with us today (Rom 7:18–25; 1 Pet 5:8–9), though as defeated foes. Consequently, Christ has won the victory, yet is in process of finalizing the victory.

This is much like our having been legally sanctified in the past by Christ's death for us (Heb 10:14), continuing to be sanctified in the present as we grow in grace (Rom 6:19–22), and finally being wholly sanctified at the resurrection when we enter our final estate (1Thess 5:23). Likewise, Scripture presents Christ's victory in three phases: He vanquishes these enemies *legally* before God's throne in his first-century redemptive work (Col 1:13–14; 2:13–15). He continues vanquishing them *historically* through the gospel's progress (Acts 26:18; 1 Cor 15:20–23). He will ultimately vanquish them *eternally* at his second advent, when he concludes history (Rom 8:18–25; Rev 20:10–15).

Thus, we see that Christ's return in great glory to effect the final judgment is necessary for completing God's redemptive plan. Otherwise sin would never finally be banished from the universe, and God would have to deal with it forever and ever, with no final concluding of the matter.

The second coming balances revealed theology in Scripture

This glorious doctrine not only finalizes Christ's redemptive victory and completes God's historical plan. But it also provides us with a full-

orbed doctrinal system balancing out majestic biblical truths. Were it not for the second advent we would:
- have a creation (Gen 1:1; Heb 11:3) without a consummation (Acts 3:20–21; Rev 20:11), resulting in an open-ended Universe (1 Cor 15:23–24; 2 Pet 3:3–4);
- have a world eternally groaning (Rom 8:22; 2 Cor 5:1–4), without any glorious perfection (Rom 8:21; 2 Pet 3:12–13);
- have a Savior quietly departing before a few of his followers (Luke 24:50–52; 1 Cor 15:5–8), without ever exhibiting his victory before all of his creatures (Rom 14:11; Phil 2:10–11);
- have a redemption spiritually focused (Rom 8:10; Eph1:3), without a physical dimension (Rom 8:11; 1 Thess 4:13–18);
- have a Redeemer bodily ascended into heaven (Acts 1:8–11; Col 2:9), without any physical (resurrected) family joining with him (1 Cor 15:20–28; Phil 3:20–21);
- have a gospel continually necessary (Matt 28:19; Acts 1:8), without any final victory (Matt 28:20; 1 Cor 15:24) — the number of the elect would never be filled.

Truly, the second coming is a "blessed hope" upon which we must carefully focus (Tit 2:13).

The Options in Eschatology

Unfortunately, evangelicals do not agree on the details of eschatology. Consequently, we also need to get our bearings regarding the different millennial views among orthodox, Bible-believing Christians. Basically four views dominate the evangelical world. Below we will briefly summarize their distinctive positions. In order to do this we must bear in mind that the labels for each system arise from Revelation 20:1–6 where John speaks of a thousand year reign of Christ (Rev 20:6).

Amillennialism

The term "amillennial" derives from a combination of Greek and Latin. It combines the Greek privative *a-* (which means "no") with the Latin adjective *mille* ("thousand") and the Latin noun *annum* ("year"). Basically the term means that the amillennial view denies a (literal) thousand year reign of Christ on earth, and that it also rejects any "millennial" conditions dominating the world before the end.

Be aware, amillennialists generally do not like this label because it presents their view in the negative and does not explain in what sense they deny a millennium. Nevertheless, we are stuck with this widely-accepted term and will be using it. The content of the system is more important than its label.

Amillennialists hold that Christ established his kingdom in the first century as a spiritual-redemptive reality and that the Church is its focal point. This kingdom will grow in history, gradually winning many converts over time as it proclaims the gospel. The present age is the "millennium," which is a symbolic value picturing a long period of time. Thus, they *do* believe in a "millennium," but of a non-literal sort.

Though the Lord's kingdom will grow, it will never achieve dominance or even a majority status in the world. In fact, it will eventually decline into wholesale apostasy as history collapses into chaos. Toward the end of history the great tribulation will erupt on the scene, opening the door to the Antichrist. Christ will then return to destroy his enemies, resurrect the dead, judge all men, and establish the eternal order.

Significantly for our purposes in developing the *post*millennial position, amillennialism is pessimistic regarding the unfolding of history toward the end. As amillennialist Cornelis Venema expresses it: "amillennialists believe that the biblical descriptions of the inter-adventual period suggests that the world's opposition to Christ and the gospel will endure, even becoming more intense as the present period of history draws to a close."[1]

Amillennialism is explained and defended in the following contemporary works by noted amillennial scholars. These can be read with much profit for understanding the position:

- Kim Riddlebarger, *A Case for Amillennialism: Understanding the End Times* (Grand Rapids: Baker, 2003).
- Cornelis P. Venema, *The Promise of the Future* (Edinburgh: Banner of Truth, 2000).

Premillennialism

The term "premillennial" derives from the compounding of three Latin terms: *prae-* ("before"), *mille* ("thousand"), and *annum* ("year"). The English prefix pre- signifies that Christ will return *before* the millennium in order to establish it.

---

[1] Cornelis Venema, *The Promise of the Future*, (Edinburgh: Banner of Truth, 2000), 239; cp. 141, 156, 242.

Premillennialists believe that Christ initiated the spiritual, anticipatory phase of his kingdom in the first century. In the kingdom's current spiritual phase God is gathering an elect people into the church. But history will eventually decline into the great tribulation when the Antichrist arises and the church apostatizes.

Not long after the arising of the Antichrist, Christ will return to resurrect deceased believers and transform living ones, fight the battle of Armageddon, and establish his one thousand year reign on the earth. During this time of his personal presence on earth, righteousness, peace, and prosperity will prevail among men. At the very end of the millennium Satan will be loosed and will prompt many to rebel against Christ. But God will intervene to destroy Satan, resurrect deceased unbelievers and transform living ones, judge all men, and establish the eternal order.

Again, since we will be presenting *post*millennialism, we should note that premillennialism is historically pessimistic. As George Eldon Ladd explains: "This evil Age is to last until His return. It will for ever be hostile to the Gospel and to God's people. Evil will prevail. . . . Persecution and martyrdom will plague the Church."[2]

Contemporary representations of premillennialism appear in the following books, which should be read for a fuller understanding of the view:

- Craig L. Blomberg and Sung Wook Chung, eds., *A Case for Historic Premillennialism: An Alternative to "Left Behind" Eschatology* (Grand Rapids: BakerAcademic, 2009).
- Gordon R. Lewis and Bruce A. Demarest, *Integrative Theology*, vol. 3: *Spirit-Given Life: God's People Present and Future* (Grand Rapids: Zondervan, 1994).

Dispensationalism

Dispensationalism is a relatively new form of premillennialism, having been created around 1830 by the Plymouth Brethren pastor and scholar, J. Nelson Darby. The term "dispensation" reflects this system's dividing history into seven distinct dispensations (i.e., eras). In each dispensation the world operates under distinguishably different God-revealed principles which are subject to distinctive divine testings, with each one ending in failure and an historical divine judgment. The present dispensation is

---

[2] George Eldon Ladd, *The Gospel of the Kingdom: Scriptural Studies in the Kingdom of God* (Grand Rapids: Eerdmans, 1959), 124.

that of Grace, which encompasses the Church Age. The next dispensation will be the last, the millennium.

Dispensationalism teaches that Christ established the Church as a new and distinct people in the first century when Israel rejected his kingdom offer. The present age is not the kingdom, but a parenthesis in the major plan of God (which focuses on Israel). Toward the end of the Church Age the world will collapse into chaos as the church apostatizes. Then Christ will return secretly (invisibly) to rapture true believers out of the world before the great tribulation. Following this the seven years of great tribulation will erupt over all the earth as the Antichrist arises to dominant the world. During this time, God will begin working with Israel once again and will receive worship through the rebuilding of the temple and the offering of blood sacrifices.

After the tribulation Christ will return visibly, bodily, and majestically (his second advent) to resurrect deceased believers and transform living ones, fight the battle of Armageddon, and establish his thousand year political reign on the earth. He will reign from Jerusalem and will be worshiped in the millennial temple by blood sacrifices. During his millennial rule righteousness, peace, and prosperity will prevail throughout the world.

At the very end of the millennium, however, Satan will be loosed and will organize a rebellion against Christ and his rule. Then God will intervene to destroy Satan, resurrect deceased unbelievers and transform living ones, judge all men, and establish the eternal order.

Once again we see the pessimistic character of an another millennial view. Indeed, dispensationalists argue "that spiritual and moral conditions in this world will get worse and worse as this present age to a close."[3] Contemporary presentations of dispensationalism (the majority view among evangelicals) include the following by noted scholars:

- Charles C. Ryrie, *Dispensationalism* (2d. ed.: Chicago: Moody, 1995).
- Norman Geisler, *Systematic Theology: Church, Last Things* (Minneapolis: Bethany, 2005).

---

[3] Paul S. Benware, *Understanding End Times Prophecy: A Comprehensive Guide* (Chicago: Moody, 1995),124.

Postmillennialism

The postmillennial view is the only option among the four eschatological systems that maintains an optimistic hope for the current age before Christ returns. The term "postmillennial" arises from the compounding of three Latin terms: *post* ("after"), *mille* ("thousand"), and *annum* ("year"). The prefix *post-* indicates that Christ will return *after* the millennium, that is, after "millennial" conditions prevail upon the earth. With amillennialism, postmillennialists understand the "thousand years" in Revelation as a symbol for an extended period of time, much like "the cattle on a thousand hills" symbolizes an enormous number of cattle (Psa 50:10) or like a thousand years of our time picturing one of God's days (Psa 90:4).

We will define postmillennialism in the next section below. Contemporary presentations of postmillennialism include:
- Kenneth L. Gentry, Jr., *He Shall Have Dominion: A Postmillennial Eschatology* (3d ed.: Draper, Vir.: ApologeticsGroup, 2009).
- Keith A. Mathison, *Postmillennialism: An Eschatology of Hope* (Phillipsburg, N.J.: Presbyterian and Reformed, 1999).

The Meaning of Postmillennialism

Since our study is explaining and defending postmillennialism, we will give a little more detailed explanation of this view.

Succinct definition

Postmillennialism holds that the Lord Jesus Christ establishes his kingdom on earth through his preaching and redemptive work in the first century. Having established the kingdom the Lord equips his church with the gospel, empowers her by the Spirit, and charges her with the Great Commission to disciple all nations.

Postmillennialism expects that eventually the vast majority of men living in the world will be saved. Increasing gospel success will gradually produce a time in history prior to Christ's return in which faith, righteousness, peace, and prosperity will prevail in the affairs of men and of nations. After an extensive era of such conditions the Lord will return visibly, bodily, and gloriously, to end history with the general resurrection and the final judgment, after which the eternal order follows.

With this brief working definition before us, we will expand on some of its key elements and implications to provide greater insights into its meaning.

Fuller explication

First, *the kingdom's first-century establishment*. Postmillennialism holds that the Lord Jesus Christ founds his Messianic kingdom on the earth during his earthly ministry and through his redemptive labors. His establishing the "kingdom of heaven" fulfills Old Testament prophetic expectations regarding the coming kingdom. The kingdom which Christ preaches and presents is not something other than that expected by the Old Testament saints. In postmillennialism the church is the fulfilled or transformed Israel and is even called "the Israel of God" (Gal 6:16).

Second, *the kingdom's fundamental nature*. It is essentially redemptive and spiritual, rather than political and corporeal. Although it has *implications* for the political realm, postmillennialism is not a political construct offering a kingdom in competition with the nations for governmental rule. Christ rules his kingdom by his Spirit working in and through his people in the world, as well as by his universal providence.

Third, *the kingdom's historical victory*. Because of the intrinsic power and design of Christ's redemptive work, his kingdom will exercise a transformational, socio-cultural influence throughout the world. This will occur as more and more people are converted to Christ. The "Christianization" of the world will not result from a revolt and seizure of political power from within history nor by the catastrophic imposition of Christ at his second advent from outside of history.

As postmillennialist R. J. Rushdoony notes in this regard: "The key to remedying the [world] situation is not revolution, nor any kind of resistance that works to subvert law and order. . . . The key is regeneration, propagation of the gospel, and the conversion of men and nations to God's law-word." This is because "evil men cannot produce a good society. The key to social renewal is individual regeneration."[4]

Fourth, *the kingdom's incremental growth*. Postmillennialism, therefore, expects the gradual, developmental expansion of Christ's kingdom in time and on earth before the Lord returns to end history. This will proceed by a full-orbed ministry of the word of God, fervent and believing prayer, and the consecrated labors of Christ's Spirit-filled people. The ever-present Christ is directing kingdom growth from his throne in heaven, where he sits at God's right hand.

---

[4] R. J. Rushdoony, *The Institutes of Biblical Law* (Vallecito, Calif.: Ross House, 1973), 113, 122.

Fifth, the *kingdom's ultimate dominance*. Postmillennialism confidently anticipates a time in earth history (continuous with the present) in which the very gospel already operating will win the victory throughout the earth, thereby fulfilling the Great Commission. Greg Bahnsen expresses this as follows: "The thing that distinguishes the biblical postmillennialist, then, from amillennialists and premillennialists is his belief that the Scripture teaches the success of the great commission in this age of the church."[5] The overwhelming majority of men and nations will be Christianized (converted and sanctified), righteousness will abound, wars will cease, and prosperity and safety will flourish.

Nineteenth-century postmillennialist David Brown expresses the final victory as follows: "It will be marked by the universal reception of the true religion, and unlimited subjection to the sceptre of Christ." "It shall be a time of universal peace." "It will be characterised by great temporal prosperity."[6]

Sixth, *the kingdom's enormous longevity*. Postmillennialist Lorraine Boettner states that: "we can look forward to a great 'golden age' of spiritual prosperity continuing for centuries, or even for millenniums, during which time Christianity shall be triumphant over all the earth."[7] After this extended period of gospel prosperity, earth history will draw to a close by the personal, visible, bodily return of Jesus Christ (accompanied by a literal resurrection and a general judgment) to introduce his blood-bought people into the consummative and eternal form of the kingdom. And so shall we ever be with the Lord.

The Optimism of Postmillennialism

Representatives of the three non-postmillennial schools do not like being called pessimistic. And we must admit that all four millennial schools are Christian systems committed to the expectation of *ultimate* redemptive hope. They unite in believing that God will finally conquer sin and Satan and establish an eternal order of glorious perfection.

---

[5] Greg L. Bahnsen, *Victory in Jesus: The Bright Hope of Postmillennialism* (Texarkana, Ark.: CMF, 1999), 74.

[6] David Brown, *Christ's Second Coming: Will It Be Premillennial?* (Edmonston, Alb.: Still Waters Revival, rep. 1990 [1882]), 399, 401.

[7] Loraine Boettner, *The Millennium* (Philadelphia: Presbyterian and Reformed, 1957), 29.

Nevertheless, they differ in how they understand the redemptive hope's impact in *history* and *before* Christ returns. Despite their agreement on the ultimate victory of God in eternity, three of the systems are *historically* pessimistic, and only one is optimistic. The three pessimistic systems are premillennialism, amillennialism, and dispensationalism.

The pessimism-optimism issue is the key matter distinguishing postmillennialism from the other three systems. But what do we mean by labeling them "pessimistic"? Those eschatologies are pessimistic in that:

- They deny that Christ's church will grow to exercise a worldwide gracious influence over the affairs of man before Christ returns.
- They deny that Christians should plan on and labor toward gospel victory in history.
- They agree that history will ultimately collapse into chaos and despair before Christ returns.

The postmillennial system is historically optimistic in that it takes the opposite position on these three issues.

Conclusion

In this *Truth About Series* study we will be presenting and explaining the biblical foundations of postmillennialism, as well as answering the leading objections to it. In establishing its biblical warrant we will focus on its most basic, defining thesis:

Christianity will continue growing throughout the world until it becomes the majority influence among men and nations, eventually leading the world into a long era of evangelical faith, personal righteousness, social peace, political stability, and economic prosperity.

With this grand outlook on history postmillennialism shows that it strongly believes that the gospel is "the power of God for salvation" (Rom 1:16). For this reason postmillennialists are firmly committed to the Great Commission which commands us: "Go therefore and make disciples of all the nations, baptizing them in the name of the Father and the Son and the Holy Spirit, teaching them to observe all that I commanded you" (Matt 28:19–20).[8]

---

[8] For a thorough exposition of the Great Commission, see: Kenneth L. Gentry, Jr., *The Greatness of the Great Commission: The Christian Enterprise in a Fallen World* (Chesnee, S.C.: Victorious Hope, 2013).

REVIEW QUESTIONS FOR DISCUSSION

These questions deal directly with the material in this chapter. The answers can be found in the chapter.
1. From where do we derive the word "eschatology"?
2. What are the two categories of eschatology? What does each involve?
3. Why is it important to understand the second coming of Christ? List the reasons given in our study. These are not the only ones; can you add some more?
4. What are the four basic eschatological positions?
5. List two key components of amillennialism and discuss how these two points distinguish this position from one of the other three.
6. List two key components of premillennialism and discuss how these two points distinguish this position from one of the other three.
7. List two key components of dispensationalism and discuss how these two points distinguish this position from one of the other three.
8. List two key components of postmillennialism and discuss how these two points distinguish this position from one of the other three.
9. What distinctive feature of postmillennialism captures its essence and distinguishes it from the other three views?
10. How are all the millennial schools optimistic? In what distinctive ways is postmillennialism optimistic in a way the other views are not?

STRETCHING FURTHER

1. Did you hold a particular millennial position before engaging this study? Which position?
2. Have you ever engaged in a systematic study of eschatology? Do you feel that you currently have a good, basic understanding of this doctrine?
3. Have you read any books that carefully present a millennial view? Name a couple of them, and tell what you thought about them.
4. What were some new ideas you learned from this chapter?
5. What do you hope to learn from our study together?

Chapter 2
POSTMILLENNIALISM IN CREATION AND COVENANT

Early in Scripture we read of both creation and covenant. Of course, creation quite naturally appears in the opening chapters of the Bible, in the book we call "Genesis." This word is taken from the Greek version of the opening of the book and basically means "birth" (and is used of such in the New Testament, Matt 1:18; Luke 1:14). Thus, Genesis is the book of births, or beginnings — especially of the world and of God's gracious covenant. Both of these concepts are important to eschatology, which deals with the conclusion of that which is begun.

The Creational Implication

In order to understand a thing aright, we must understand its purpose according to its designer. Eschatology is the doctrine concerned with the end of history, and therefore deals with the divinely revealed, long-range purpose of the world. Thus, creation and eschatology are logically linked, as the beginning and the end.

For our eschatological study, we may discover the postmillennial hope at the very beginning of Scripture and history, for it is implicit in the creation and fall narratives themselves. Let us see how this is so.

The creation narrative

As Christians we believe that "in the beginning God created the heavens and the earth" (Gen 1:1; cp. Exo 20:11; 31:17; Psa 102:25). We worship him who is "the everlasting God, the LORD, the *Creator* of the ends of the earth" (Isa 40:28). Therefore, we understand that we live in a rational world because it was created by a rational God. The rational world is not rooted in irrational Chance, as per the secular and naturalistic views of origins.

God's revelation in Scripture also teaches us that God does everything according to his own purpose. He made the world by the exercise of his wisdom (Psa 104:24; cp. Psa 136:5; Jer 10:12; 51:15). And he "works all things after the counsel of His will" (Eph 1:11). And since he is the "everlasting God" (Isa 40:28), his purpose "will be established" (Isa 46:10), it truly "stands forever" (Psa 33:11; Prov 19:21; Isa 14:24). Consequently, the world has meaning, purpose, and significance.

Now since God "created the heavens and the earth" after "the counsel of His will," we must ask: Why? Why did God create "the world and all things in it" (Acts 17:24)? For what purpose did he establish the material realm in which we live?

As evangelical Christians we believe God is good (Psa 86:5; 100:5; 106:1; 119:68; Jer 33:11; Nah 1:7) and that he created all things good (Gen 1:31; 1 Tim 4:4). We also believe that our good God created all things to bring glory to himself. The heavenly hosts praise him for his creative glory: "Worthy are You, our Lord and our God, to receive glory and honor and power; *for* You created *all things*, and because of Your will they existed, and were created" (Rev 4:11). We may surmise that our good God created a good world for his own glory with the intent of bringing positive good from his world.

What is more, our good God not only created all things good, but he created man in his image (Gen 1:26–27; cp. Gen 9:6). An important aspect of the multi-faceted image of God in man is our reflecting God's dominion over creation. We see this emphasized when God declared that he would create man in his image: "Then God said, 'Let Us make man in Our image, according to Our likeness; *and let them rule over* the fish of the sea and over the birds of the sky and over the cattle and over all the earth, and over every creeping thing that creeps on the earth'" (Gen 1:26).

Thus, the image of the creator God, which is emphasized in the context of the creation process itself, involves man's authority to exercise rule over the rest of creation. *Man was created to rule the world to the glory of God.*

Later in the Psalms, David praises God when he reflects on his creating man with such authority over all creation:

"What is man that You take thought of him, / And the son of man that You care for him? / Yet You have made him a little lower than God, / And You crown him with glory and majesty! / You make him to rule over the works of Your hands; / You have put all things under his feet, / All sheep and oxen, / And also the beasts of the field, / The birds of the heavens and the fish of the sea, / Whatever passes through the paths of the seas. / O LORD, our Lord, / How majestic is Your name in all the earth!" (Psa 8:4-9)

David was humbled by the fact of God's creating man and commissioning him to exercise dominion in God's world and under God's rule.

We must understand that at the very beginning God does *not* create man as *possessing* the image of God — as if it were an *added quality* which man could lose. He does not *imbue* man with his image by bestowing it on him *after* his creation. Rather, he creates man *as* his image, so that man *is* inherently the image of God *by definition*. God's image constitutes the very nature of man *as man*. From the very beginning man *is* the image of God.

Thus, God created man to reflect (on a creaturely level) God's own creative power and rulership authority over the world. And man remains God's image even after his fall into sin, for we read later of fallen man: "Whoever sheds man's blood, / By man his blood shall be shed, / For in the image of God / He made man" (Gen 9:6). Psalm 8 also shows that man's call to dominion remains after the fall. Of course, we should expect this since man inherently *is* God's image, and the image of God expressly reflects God's ultimate dominion.

So we see that God created man as a dominion creature a commissioned him with the "Cultural Mandate" (Gen 1:26) to subdue the earth to the glory of God. The question arises then: Will man subdue the earth to God's glory as God intended? That is, will God's creational purpose for man be realized — *in history*? Postmillennialism declares that it will. The fact that it is repeated later in biblical history demands that we recognize that God still intends to see it accomplished by man's labor in the world.

As an optimistic eschatology postmillennialism seeks the transformation of all human culture for God's glory. Postmillennialism is strongly committed to the fact that "the earth is the Lord's, and all it contains, / The world, and those who dwell in it" (Psa 24:1). This declaration is a constant refrain throughout Scripture, as we see in Exodus 9:29; 19:5; Leviticus 25:23; Deuteronomy 10:14; 1 Samuel 2:8; 1 Chronicles 29:11, 14; Job 41:11; Psalm 50:12; 89:11; 104:24; and 1 Cor 10:26.

Postmillennialism embodies a Bible-based, world-encompassing outlook — a truly Christian worldview. In fact, it establishes an *optimistic* worldview confidently expecting God's promise will come true: "indeed, as I live, all the earth will be filled with the glory of the Lord" (Num 14:21). We may trace the roots of this optimistic worldview back to the very creation account.

But what about man's fall into sin? Does this not seem to undermine the postmillennialism's optimistic expectation? Ironically the record of Adam's fall actually underscores this hope. So let us now consider:

The fall narrative

God does not give up on man when Adam falls into sin. In fact, immediately after the fall God reveals his plan for redeeming man. And he designs this redemption ultimately to secure what we call "the postmillennial hope."

When God approaches Adam and Eve after the fall, he declares what scholars have called the *protoevangelium*, "the first promise of the gospel." In Genesis 3:15 we read of God's curse on Satan through the serpent, who is later called "the serpent of old" (Rev 12:9; 20:2). In this we discover God promising that Satan will be crushed by the coming Redeemer (the seed of the woman, Christ):

"And I will put enmity / Between you and the woman, / And between your seed and her seed; / He shall bruise you on the head, / And you shall bruise him on the heel."

The record of the fall and God's response to it exhibit an important eschatological angle. To properly grasp this, we must first understand that: God created man as an *historical* creature from the very dust of the earth (Gen 2:7[9]); that Satan appeared to Adam as an historical creature (the serpent, Gen 3:1) in the context of history (Gen 3:1–5); that the fall involved historical realities (the tree that God created, Gen 2:16–17; 3:2–3); that the fall would have historical consequences (the enmity and struggle between the two seeds, Gen 3:15); and that the Redeemer would come in the context of history (the New Testament record presents Christ as the fulfillment of this redemptive expectation, Mt 13:17; Gal 4:4).

Now since all of these features of the fall narrative are historical, why should we not expect that the crushing of Satan would also be historical and lead to historical results? In fact, postmillennialism does expect such. Though Genesis 3:15 forecasts the *struggle* between Christ and Satan in history, we must recognize that its main point is actually the *victory* of Christ over Satan.

---

[9] Tragically some Christians are so heavenly-minded that they are of no earthly good, denigrating the material realm in extolling the spiritual. But we must recognize how much God values the material order for he: (1) created it (Gen 1; Psa 33:6–11); (2) gave us physical bodies (Gen 2:7–24); (3) commissioned us to serve in it (Gen 1:26–27); (4) took upon himself a true human body to redeem us (Rom 1:3; 9:5; Heb 2:14); and destines us to a material new creation order (2 Pet 3:8–13).

Postmillennialism holds that Christ's redemptive work is more powerful than Adam's sinful fall. Postmillennialists believe that redemption was not only designed to overcome the effects of the fall in history, but actually does so. After all, are you not saved from the fall? Your redemption is a subtle declaration of the postmillennial hope. If God can save you, he can save others.

The Covenantal Promise

Moving a little further into biblical history, we come upon God's covenant with Abraham. The Abrahamic Covenant is a major redemptive divine covenant. In fact, it is foundational to redemption and the messianic hope, as we see from the New Testament repeatedly mentioning it (Luke 1:55, 73; Acts 3:25; Rom 4:12–16; Gal 3:6–18). The essence of the Abrahamic Covenant appears in Genesis 12:2–3 (cp. Gen 15:5–7):

"I will make you a great nation, / And I will bless you, / And make your name great; / And so you shall be a blessing; / And I will bless those who bless you, / And the one who

curses you I will curse. / And in you all the families of the earth shall be blessed."

This glorious covenant has powerful implications for our present eschatological study. It clearly declares that "*all peoples on earth* will be blessed through" Abraham. In fact, through it we as Christians become heirs of Abraham: "If you belong to Christ, then you are Abraham's offspring, heirs according to promise" (Gal 3:29; cp. Rom 4:12–13, 16; Gal 3:7–9, 14).

Thus, the consequence of God's redemptive promise ultimately will include "all the families of the earth." The Hebrew word for "families" here includes nations. The Abrahamic Covenant will include the families — or, more properly, nations — beyond Israel. The ultimate purpose of this covenant is nothing less than world conversion, rather than Israel exaltation, as per dispensationalism. We should expect this since the Lord is King of the whole earth and desires the world to know Him (Psa 2:8; 22:27; 66:4; 86:9).

Paul explains that "the Scripture, foreseeing that God would justify the *Gentiles* by faith, preached the *gospel* beforehand to Abraham, saying, '*All the nations* shall be blessed in you'" (Gal 3:8). Elsewhere he emphasizes the global glory of the Abrahamic Covenant, when he declares that "the promise" to Abraham is that "he would be heir of the *world*" (Rom 4:13).

This expectation of worldwide victory is so strong that we find in later Scriptures repeated casual references to it. For instance, Abraham's seed is to "possess the gates of the enemy" (Gen 22:17 cp. Matt 16:18). Genesis 49:8–10 promises that Judah will maintain the scepter of rule until Shiloh [Christ] shall come, and then to him "shall be the obedience of the peoples." We should note the plural "peoples." Shiloh's winning of obedience is not among the Jews only (the people, singular). Ezekiel and Paul both allude to this with confidence — Ezekiel in anticipation (Eze 21:27), Paul in realization (Gal 3:19).

Numbers 14:21 confirms the victorious expectation with a formulaic oath: "Truly, as I live, all the earth shall be filled with the glory of the LORD." In Numbers 24:17–19 Balaam harkens back to Jacob's prophecy in Genesis 49:10. He foresees an all-powerful, world-wide dominion for the Messiah:

"A star shall come forth from Jacob, and a scepter shall rise from Israel, and shall crush through the forehead of Moab, and tear down all the sons of Sheth. And Edom shall be a possession, Seir, its enemies, also shall be a possession, while Israel performs valiantly. One from Jacob shall have dominion, and shall destroy the remnant from the city."

First Samuel 2:10 promises that "Those who contend with the LORD will be shattered; / Against them He will thunder in the heavens, / The LORD will judge the ends of the earth; / And He will give strength to His king, / And will exalt the horn of His anointed." Thus, as noted above, the New Testament declares: "For the promise that he would be the *heir of the world* was not to Abraham or to his seed through the law, but through the righteousness of faith" (Rom 4:13).

All of this supports the postmillennialist's historical optimism. Abraham's promised heirship of the world comes by means of the spread of the gospel. We would point out also that the historical prospects of gospel victory bringing blessing upon all nations comes *by gradualistic conversion*. It does not come by catastrophic imposition, as in premillennialism where Christ personally and directly imposes his political rule through the battle of Armageddon. Nor does it come by apocalyptic-conclusion, as in amillennialism wherein Christ personally and directly wins the victory at the last moment of history in his consummational second coming to set up the eternal order.

The optimistic historical goal of the Abrahamic Covenant shines through clearly in the prophets, to which we will turn in our next chapter.

Conclusion

We have seen that both creation and covenant are significant features of the postmillennial system. And divine revelation regarding both occur in the first book of the Bible, and thus very early in its historical record.

The foundational book of all of Scripture presents the postmillennial hope. In Genesis, the book of beginnings, we find the creation of the world and man for God's glory (Gen 1), the commissioning of man as God's image (Gen 1:26–28), the beginning of sin and God's response in redemption (Gen 3), and the covenantal framework for worldwide salvation (Gen 12). And in each of these we see the postmillennial hope shining brightly.

REVIEW QUESTIONS FOR DISCUSSION

These questions deal directly with the material in this chapter. The answers can be found in the chapter.

1. How is eschatology logically linked to creation?
2. What is it about God's creating the world that suggests our postmillennial theme of optimism for history?
3. What defines man as man, distinguishing him from the animals? How does this suggest hope for human culture and society?
4. What does Cultural Mandate in Genesis 1:26–28 teach? How is this helpful to postmillennialism?
5. When Adam sinned, God banished him from Eden. Did God withdraw or disannul the Cultural Mandate after Adam rebelled against him in Eden? Provide evidence for your answer.
6. Man's fall into sin seems to derail any hope for man in history. What feature of the fall narrative in Genesis 3 suggests to the postmillennialist a hope for future progress *in history*?
7. The Abrahamic Covenant obviously was made with Abraham and is the basis of God's Old Testament blessings on Israel. But was the Abrahamic Covenant for Israel alone? Prove your answer from Scripture.
8. How does the Abrahamic Covenant impact the Christian's hope for the future? How do we see this in its Old Testament revelation? In its New Testament mention?
9. Most passages presenting an optimistic view of history are rooted in direct prophetic insights into the future. Some hope-filled expectations, however, are based on God's solemn oath. Can you cite any

passages that present this hope in a divine-oath format? How is this particularly significant for an eschatological position?
10. How do the four millennial positions differ regarding their understanding of the coming of kingdom victory? That is, each system has some form of optimism regarding God's kingdom, but they see its method of victory differently. How do those methods differ?

STRETCHING FURTHER

1. Had you ever thought of creation and its relationship to eschatology?
2. Since we as Christians worship a spiritual God and are eventually to go to heaven to be with him, do we have any real interest in the material world and the historical order? What makes you answer in this way?
3. We read of the seed of the woman in Genesis 3:15 and Abraham's seed in Genesis 22:18. How are these two seeds related? To what do they ultimate point?
4. What is the biblical idea of covenant?
5. What were some new ideas you learned from this chapter?

Chapter 3
POSTMILLENNIALISM IN THE PSALMS AND PROPHETS

In our study of postmillennialism, we are focusing on its most distinctive feature, that element which separates it from each of the other evangelical eschatologies: optimism for the future, the confident hope for man's righteous progress in history. Our optimism for the future does not depend on human wisdom or man's nature, for both are corrupted by sin. Rather, it depends on God and his saving mercies in Christ.

So far we have seen that the postmillennial hope is rooted in creation and covenant. That is, our hope as Christians flows out of God's creative purpose and through his redemptive covenant. God created this world for his own glory and will not give up on it. He created man in his own image and called him to a glorious task of righteous cultural development, and he never withdrew that call. In fact, he re-established it by beginning the process of redemption. His redemptive program calls for the conquest of Satan in history, and is controlled by his gracious covenant through Abraham.

We will now move into Scriptures that are more obviously prophetic in nature and intent. In the first section below we will consider the glorious, hope-filled Messianic Psalms. Then we will focus on the writing prophets. Obviously these overtly prophetic materials are important to the eschatological debate. The amount of material in the numerous prophetic psalms and the writing prophets, however, is too large for us to consider in our succinct *Truth About Series* presentation.[1] Consequently, we will succinctly highlight just a few of them. Their clarity should easily confirm the postmillennial outlook.

The Psalms and Hope

The Messianic Psalms are dearly loved by all Christians. But they are poorly understood by most Christians. Despite the prevailing historical pessimism of the three other eschatological schools (amillennialism, premillennialism, dispensationalism), these psalms greatly encourage the

---

[1] For a thorough, 600-page treatment, see: Kenneth L. Gentry, Jr.. *He Shall Have Dominion: A Postmillennial Eschatology* (Draper, Vir.: ApologeticsGroup, 2009).

postmillennialist's optimism for the historical long-run. Let us see how this is so.

A quick survey of the Messianic Psalms

Obviously space and time constraints forbid analyzing each and every prophetic announcement in the Psalms. But we can gain some insights even from a quick survey of a few of them.

For instance, Psalm 22 anticipates a time when "all the ends of the earth will remember and turn to the LORD, / And all the families of the nations will worship before You" (Psa 22:27). This obviously anticipates evangelistic success among the nations due to the gospel, rather than Armageddon imposition upon the nations due to the second advent. The "remembering" here undoubtedly refers to the fact that God created man, and in their conversion they will recall this.

Psalm 66 reflects this hope, promising that "all the earth will worship You / And will sing praises to You / They will sing praises to Your name" (Psa 66:4). This prophecy is preceded by the universal command: "Shout joyfully to God, all the earth; / Sing the glory of His name; / Make His praise glorious" (Psa 66:1). And as a consequence of this prophetic expectation, the Psalm continues with a further command: "Bless our God, O peoples, /And sound His praise abroad" (Psa 66:8).

Other psalms praise God that his saving work will be effected among the nations. The psalmist anticipates "that Your way may be known on the earth, / Your salvation among all nations" (Psa 67:2). In fact, he continues with a command on this basis: "Let the peoples praise You, O God; / Let all the peoples praise You. / Let the nations be glad and sing for joy; / For You will judge the peoples with uprightness / And guide the nations on the earth. / Let the peoples praise You, O God; / Let all the peoples praise You" (Psa 67:3–5). He sees that God's blessings on Israel are ultimately so that "all the ends of the earth may fear him" (Psa 67:7).

Elsewhere the psalms promise that "all nations whom Thou hast made shall come and worship before You O Lord" (Psa 86:9). Even renowned enemies will be converted, such as Rahab, Babylon, Philistia, Tyre, and Ethiopia (Psa 87:4). Indeed, all nations and kings will revere him (Psa 102:15).

In fact, the most important prophetic psalm in the Old Testament declares that Christ will be seated at God's right hand until all of his enemies become his footstool (Psa 110:1). This dramatic declaration is so important that it becomes the most cited Old Testament verse found in the New Testament.[2] Note that his enemies become his footstool *while he is seated at God's right hand* (where he appears after his ascension: Acts 2:33–35; 5:31; 7:56; Rom 8:34; Eph 1:20; Col 3:1; Heb 1:3, 13; 8:1; 10:12; 12:2; 1 Pet 3:22) — not *after* leaving that place and *returning to earth* at his second coming. Again, his victory will occur in contemporary history as Christ presently rules from heaven.

In Psalm 72 Messianic victory is associate with pre-consummational history, *before* the renovation of the present universe and the establishment of the eternal New Heavens and Earth:

"Let them fear Thee *while* the sun endures, / And *as long as* the moon, throughout all generations. / May he come down like rain upon the mown grass, / Like showers that water the earth. / In his days may the righteous flourish, / And abundance of peace *till* the moon is no more. / May he also rule from sea to sea, / And from the River to the ends of the earth."(Psa 72:5–8)

Now let us consider more closely a particularly significant psalm for our presentation of the postmillennial hope: Psalm 2.

A careful study of a Messianic Psalm

Psalm 2 may be second only to Psalm 110 for its influence on the New Testament writers. It is either cited or clearly alluded to in Matt 3:17; 17:5; Mark 1:11; 9:7; Luke 3:22; 9:35; Phil 2:11; Rev 2:26–27; 11:18; and 19:19. And as with each of the preceding psalms, we once again find another inspired, optimistic outlook on history. It recognizes the turmoil among the nations, but ends with God's kingdom winning the victory. Thus, it follows the two-step progress of the *protoevangelium* (Gen 3:15): temporal struggle followed by historical victory.

This psalm opens with the nations raging "against the Lord and against His Anointed One " (Psa 2:1–3) . The term "Anointed One" is the Hebrew word "messiah," which speaks of the Deliverer whom the Jews long expected (see: John 1:20, 24–25, 41, 49; cp. Mark 15:32; Luke 24: 19–21). As the New Testament teaches, he is none other than the Lord Jesus Christ (Mark 8:29-30; 14:61–62). In fact, the word "Christ" is the Greek translation of the Hebrew word "Messiah."

---

[2] Quotations include: Matt 22:44; 26:64; Mark 12:36; 14:62; Luke 20:42–43; 22:69; Acts 2:34–35; Heb 1:13. Allusions may be found in: 1 Cor 15:24; Eph 1:20–22; Phil 2:9–11; Heb 1:3; 8:1; 10:12, 13; 1 Pet 3:22; Rev 3:21.

In the psalm we see the nations sinfully plotting and struggling to free themselves from the reign of the Lord and his Anointed: "Let us tear their fetters apart, / And cast away their cords from us!" (Psa 2:3). Ultimately though, we learn that their rage is not only evil but futile. For the Lord sits serenely enthroned in majesty above: "He who sits in the heavens laughs, / The Lord scoffs at them" (Psa 2:4).

Not only does the New Testament interpret this psalm messianicly, but associates the rage of the nations with the first-century crucifixion of Jesus:

> "The Holy Spirit, through the mouth of our father David Your servant, said, / Why did the Gentiles rage, / And the peoples devise futile things? / The kings of the earth took their stand, / And the rulers were gathered together / Against the Lord, and against His Christ. For truly in this city there were gathered together against Your holy servant Jesus, whom You anointed, both Herod and Pontius Pilate, along with the Gentiles and the peoples of Israel." (Acts 4:25–27)

In Psalm 2:5 God's long-suffering confidence finally gives way to his righteous indignation: "Then He will speak to them in His anger / And terrify them in His fury" (Psa 2:5). Significantly, commentators note that Psalm 2 borrows from Exodus 15, where Moses' song of celebration recounts God's defeat of Egypt at the Exodus and anticipates the future terror of Israel's enemies, the Canaanites. Since Psalm 2 is Messianic and ultimately refers to Christ, it teaches that he will conquer the raging nations of the world just as surely as God conquers Israel's Old Testament foes.

In contrast to the nations' raging futility, God sovereignly declares: "But as for me [emphatic personal pronoun in the Hebrew], I have installed My King / Upon Zion, My holy mountain" (Psa 2:6). God does not speak of this installed one as "a king" or "the king," but as "*My* King." Verse 7 expands on this installation, as the Messiah himself speaks: "I will surely tell of the decree of the Lord: / He said to me, 'You are My Son; / Today I have begotten You." The "decree" is a pledge of adoption by God: "You are My Son; / Today I have begotten You." It serves as a holy coronation rite establishing this King's legitimacy (see: 2 Sam 7:13–14; Psa 89:26–27).

As we look at this Psalm, we must note the word "today." It suggests a moment at which the title is associated with the new ruler. And this is important to the postmillennial argument. Rather than this installation occurring at Christ's second advent, as many Christians assume, the New Testament relates it once again to the first century: at the exaltation of Christ which begins with his resurrection. "God has fulfilled this promise to our children in that He raised up Jesus, as it is also written in the second Psalm, 'You are My Son; today I have begotten You'" (Acts 13:33).

Consequently, we must understand that since his resurrection and ascension Christ has been installed as the King (Rom 1:4), ruling from God's right hand (Rom 14:9–11; Eph 1:20ff; Col 1:18; 1 Pet 3:22; Rev 17: 14; 19:16). In a later chapter We will note that the Great Commission speaks of Christ's being "given" all authority at this very point in time (Matt 28:18; cp. Phil 2:9).

Now we must ask what the Psalm means when it speaks of his installation "on Zion"? Zion is an historical site in the "City of David" (2 Sam 5:6–9). After David brought the Ark to Zion, the hill became sacred (2 Sam 6:10–12). Because of its significance in old covenant history, the name "Zion" gradually began to be applied beyond the historical site to include Mount Moriah where Solomon builds the Temple (Isa 8:18; Joel 3:17; Mic 4:7). Eventually it covers all of Jerusalem (2 Kgs 19:21; Psa 48:2, 11–13; 69:35; Isa 1:8), even representing the whole Jewish nation (Isa 40:9; Zech 9:13).

Zion, therefore, becomes a symbol of God's presence and rule in the world. New Testament writers use Zion and Jerusalem as symbols that transcend Old Testament realities. In fact, these historical settings are applied to heaven itself. Hebrews puts the matter quite clearly when writing to first-century Jewish Christians: "But you have come to *Mount Zion* and to the city of the living God, the *heavenly Jerusalem*, and to myriads of angels" (Heb 12:22; cp. Gal 4:25–26; Rev 14:1). Thus, the New Testament sees the center of divine rule being transferred to heaven, where Christ currently rules over his kingdom, for his kingdom is not of this world (John 18:36; cp. Rev 1:5).

According to the psalm, God promises his Messiah: "Ask of me, and I will surely give the nations as Your inheritance, / And the very ends of the earth as Your possession" (Psa 2:8). Remarkably, this securing of "the nations" is the very task he assigns to his followers in the Great Commission: "Go and make disciples of all nations" (Matt 28:19). He will rule over them with his rod and dash in pieces those who refuse to submit (Psa 2:9). This he does by "the word of his power" while" at the right hand of the Majesty on high" (Heb 1:3; cp. Heb 8–13; Matt 21:43–44).

Because of this ultimate hope, the psalmist issues a warning to the nations:

"Now therefore, O kings, show discernment; / Take warning, O judges of the earth. / Worship the Lord with reverence, / And rejoice with trembling. / Do homage to the Son, lest He become angry, and you perish in the way, / For His wrath may soon be kindled. / How blessed are all who take refuge in Him!" (Psa 2:10–12)

Thus, we see that Psalm 2 continues developing the twin redemptive-historical themes of struggle and victory which began with the redemptive promise to Adam (see ch. 2 above). It throbs with historical optimism and serves virtually as a postmillennial tract.

Let us now turn to the prophets, where we will discover this tendency continuing.

The Prophets and Hope

Obviously, if postmillennialism is biblically-based we should expect to find it's radiant optimism shining in the Old Testament prophets. And we certainly do. We will quickly cite a few samples from the writing prophets, then focus in more detail on one particularly powerful sample from the greatest of the writing prophets, Isaiah.

A brief prophecy sampling

Isaiah 9:6–7. This Isaianic prophecy is one of the more familiar passages in the Old Testament:

"For a child will be born to us, a son will be given to us; / And the government will rest on His shoulders; / And His name will be called Wonderful Counselor, Mighty God, Eternal Father, Prince of Peace. / There will be no end to the increase of His government or of peace, / On the throne of David and over his kingdom, / To establish it and to uphold it with justice and righteousness / From then on and forevermore. / The zeal of the LORD of hosts will accomplish this."

Here we find the promise that "a child will be born to us" (Isa 9:6a). All Christians recognize that this refers to the birth of Christ. But there is more here than we often recognize.

Though this passage presents the Lord's birth, it then immediately points to *purpose* of his birth: he was born to rule: "the government will rest on His shoulders" (Isa 9:6b). This is obviously speaking of the coming of the Messianic kingdom for it focuses on "the throne of David" (Isa 9:7b).

The government that rests on his shoulders, however, is not to be a literal, bureaucratic, political kingdom. We know this from the New Testament's development of the Davidic kingdom. For instance, in Acts 2: 29–35 Peter preaches at Pentecost that at his resurrection and ascension Christ fulfills the Davidic promise:

"Brethren, I may confidently say to you regarding the patriarch David that he both died and was buried, and his tomb is with us to this day. And so, because he was a prophet and knew that God had sworn to him with an oath to seat one of his descendants on his throne, he looked ahead and spoke of the resurrection of the Christ, that He was neither abandoned to hades, nor did His flesh suffer decay. This Jesus God raised up again, to which we are all witnesses. Therefore having been exalted to the right hand of God, and having received from the Father the promise of the Holy Spirit, He has poured forth this which you both see and hear. For it was not David who ascended into heaven, but he himself says: 'the Lord said to my lord, 'sit at my right hand, until I make your enemies a footstool for your feet.'"

Peter's proclamation of the Davidic kingdom is strongly postmillennial in complexion: (1) The promise that David's descendant would sit on his throne is a promise of Christ's resurrection (Acts 2:30–31), which has already happened (Acts 2:32, 36). (2) Christ's enthronement is not an earthly one, but is at "the right hand of God" (Acts 2:33) which is in heaven (Acts 2:34; cp. John 18:37). (3) He is seated in heaven until they become "a footstool for [his] feet" (Acts 2:35), i.e., until after he defeats all of his enemies in history.

Returning now to Isaiah's prophecy, we may note that it speaks in a postmillennial fashion. It declares that his "government" will bring "peace" (Isa 9:7a). And that this peace will be established in "justice and righteousness" (Isa 9:7c).

Quite importantly too, Isaiah also speaks of his government as growing gradually over time: "there will be no end to the *increase* of His government or of peace" (Isa 9:7a). Thus, his prophesied kingdom will not appear full blown in catastrophic imposition, as expected in dispensationalism. Rather, it will "increase," grow and develop incrementally. Later Jesus teaches that his kingdom will grow slowly like a mustard seed and like leaven (Matt 13:31–33).

Isaiah is confident in the growth of Christ's kingdom. It is certain for "the zeal of the Lord of hosts will accomplish this" (Isa 9:7e).

Isaiah 11. In Isaiah 11 we find another Messianic prophecy that highlights the gradualistic nature of Christ's kingdom and its ultimate victory. Christ will appear in history as a mere "shoot" that springs from the "stem of Jesse," a "branch" that "will bear fruit" (Isa 11:1). Yet because of his coming, earth's future is glorious: "They shall not hurt nor destroy in all My holy mountain, for the earth shall be full of the knowledge of the LORD as the waters cover the sea" (Isa 11:9).

But again we must notice that glorious result will unfold *gradually*, beginning "in that day" when the "root of Jesse" shall stand as a banner (signal, place of rendezvous) to "the nations" (Isa 11:10) followed by the conversion of the Jews (Isa 11:11). The first-century calling of the Gentiles certainly shows the fulfillment of verse 10 is underway. And that calling continues even to this very day (Rom 15:4–12, see especially v 12). As Paul teaches, the future conversion of the Jews will conclude the kingdom's growth in history: "a partial hardening has happened to Israel until the fullness of the Gentiles has come in; and so all Israel will be saved" (Rom 11:12–25; see ch. 5 below).

Jeremiah 31:33–34. God promises through Jeremiah the coming of the new covenant. This is the covenant which Christ establishes just before his crucifixion as he institutes the Lord's Supper: "This cup which is poured out for you is the new covenant in My blood" (Luke 22:20b; 1 Cor 11:25). According to God's revelation to Jeremiah, as a result of the new covenant: "'they shall not teach again, each man his neighbor and each man his brother, saying, "Know the Lord," for they shall all know Me, from the least of them to the greatest of them,' declares the Lord, 'for I will forgive their iniquity, and their sin I will remember no more'" (Jer 31:34).

Supplementing this new covenant hope, Jeremiah foresees the day when no one will even remember the ark of the covenant as the local presence of the Lord. This is because "all the nations will be gathered before" the "throne of the Lord" (Jer 3:16–17). He envisions a time in which the historical enemies of God's people will be blessed, including Moab (Jer 48:47), Ammon (Jer 49:6), and Elam (Jer 49:39). This matches a dramatic prophecy in Isaiah:

"In that day there will be a highway from Egypt to Assyria, and
the Assyrians will come into Egypt and the Egyptians into Assyria,
and the Egyptians will worship with the Assyrians. In that day

Israel will be the third party with Egypt and Assyria, a blessing in the midst of the earth, whom the Lord of hosts has blessed, saying, 'Blessed is Egypt My people, and Assyria the work of My hands, and Israel My inheritance.'" (Isa 19:23–25)

Other prophecies. Many other prophecies foresee a future of worldwide blessing. Among the many available to us are the following few samples.

- Daniel 7:14 presents a vision of the future in which "to Him was given dominion, / Glory and a kingdom, / That all the peoples, nations, and men of every language / Might serve Him. / His dominion is an everlasting dominion / Which will not pass away; / And His kingdom is one / Which will not be destroyed.."
- Amos 9:12 mentions "all the nations who are called by My name." Those days will witness abundant harvests and prosperity (Amos 9:13).
- Micah 5:4 (another Christmas passage, see v 2) promises that Christ "will be great / To the ends of the earth."
- Habakkuk 2:14 declares that "the earth will be filled / With the knowledge of the glory of the Lord, / As the waters cover the sea."
- Zechariah 9:9–10 presents Christ, whose "dominion will be from sea to sea, / And from the River to the ends of the earth." Later he states: "And the Lord will be king over all the earth; in that day the Lord will be the only one, and His name the only one" (Zech 14:9).
- Malachi 1:11 declares that "My name will be great among the nations, and in every place incense is going to be offered to My name, and a grain offering that is pure; for My name will be great among the nations."

On and on we could go: the prophetic writings are filled with *optimism* regarding the *growth* of God's kingdom and Christ's victory *in history*. The Lord explains to the Emmaus Road disciples that he suffered so that he might enter into his glory: "'Was it not necessary for the Christ to suffer these things and to enter into His glory?' Then beginning with Moses and with all the prophets, He explained to them the things concerning Himself in all the Scriptures" (Luke 24:26).

A focused prophecy study

Isaiah is a large work, often lovingly called "the Gospel of Isaiah." The name "Isaiah" itself means "salvation is of the LORD." In this book of prophecy's we find much hope regarding the victory of the gospel message.

One of Isaiah's earliest prophecies powerfully declares God's victory in the world. And it follows the pattern already set by the *protoevangelium* (Gen 3:15), the Abrahamic Covenant (Gen 12:2–3), and the messianic psalms (Psa 2; 22; 66; 67; 110; etc.). Isaiah's prophecy in 2:2–4 reads:

> "Now it will come about that / In the last days, / The mountain of the house of the Lord / Will be established as the chief of the mountains, / And will be raised above the hills; / And all the nations will stream to it. / And many peoples will come and say, "Come, let us go up to the mountain of the Lord, / To the house of the God of Jacob; / That He may teach us concerning His ways, / And that we may walk in His paths." / For the law will go forth from Zion, / And the word of the Lord from Jerusalem. / And He will judge between the nations, / And will render decisions for many peoples; / And they will hammer their swords into plowshares, and their spears into pruning hooks. / Nation will not lift up sword against nation, / And never again will they learn war."

Interestingly, Isaiah 2 is repeated almost verbatim by Micah (Mic 4:1–3). Let's consider some of the key elements of this duplicated prophecy.

"In the last days." Before we can consider the glorious expectations in this prophecy, we mst begin by considering when these events will occur. Isaiah opens his prophecy by presenting its time frame: "in the last days" (Isa 2:2b). But the question arises: *"When* do the last days occur?"

Many Christians today think the "last days" either started in 1948 when Israel became a nation once again or that they will soon start in our near future. But the New Testament answers the question much differently: the "last days" begin in the first century, i.e., in the apostolic era (e.g., 1 Cor 10:11; Heb 9:26; 1 John 2:18; 1 Pet 1:20).

In fact, the Spirit's outpouring at Pentecost formally initiates the "last days." Peter explains the experience at that particular Pentecost for his original audience: "This is what was spoken of through the prophet Joel: 'And it shall be *in the last days*'" (Acts 2:16–17a). He is declaring to all those gathered at Pentecost that the outbreak of tongues-speaking is a sign that the last days have come.[3]

Theologically-speaking, history is divided between the former days (before Christ) and the "last days" (after Christ). Hebrews puts it this way: "God, after He spoke long ago to the fathers in the prophets in many portions and in many ways, in *these last days* has spoken to us in His Son" (Heb 1:1–2a).

The "last days" not only begin in the first century but they continue through the remaining days of history until the second coming of Christ. Christ's second advent will mark "the end," for as Paul puts it: "at His coming, then comes the end" (1 Cor 15:24; cp. Matt 13:39–40, 49). At that time he will resurrect the dead — because "the *last* day" has arrived: "No one can come to Me unless the Father who sent Me draws him; and I will raise h im up on the last day" (John 6:44, cp. John 6:39, 54; 11:24; 12:48). Obviously, the "last day" occurs at the end of the series of "last days."

This has important theological implications for us. *The days in which we have been living since the first century are "the last days."* And since these are the "last" days, no more days are to follow — otherwise these would not be "the *last* days." Consequently, we should not expect a thousand years — or 365,000 days! — to follow. That is, we cannot hold to a future millennium (1000 years) after Christ secretly raptures the church and resurrects those who are saved. Because he himself teaches us that when he resurrects his own it *is* the last day. No days follow the *last* day. This stands strongly against dispensationalism.

So then, Isaiah introduces his prophecy by declaring that the "last days" will be the era witnessing the results contained within — not some era *after* the last days. "*In* the last days" (Isa 2:2) means "during," i.e., while the last days are still unfolding. But what is to occur "in the last days"?

"The mountain of the house of the Lord." Isaiah expects that the "mountain of the house of the Lord" will be "established as the chief of the mountains, / And will be raised above the hills" (Isa 2:2c, d). This obviously is not to be understood literally, for two reasons: (1) Any physical raising up of the "mountain" would involve massive tectonic up-thrusting which would destroy this "house of the Lord." (2) And if it were physically

---

[3] See: Kenneth L. Gentry, Jr., *Tongues-Speaking: The Meaning, Purpose, and Cessation of Tongues* (Chesnee, S.C.: Victorious Hope, 2014), chs. 4 and 5.

raised up to be "the chief of the mountains," it would be absolutely uninhabitable as a location higher than the Himalayan Mountains.

Rather, this speaks of the exaltation and prominence of the "mountain of the house of the Lord," i.e., the temple of God. In the New Testament the literal temple system is spoken of as vanishing away: "When He said, 'A new covenant,' He has made the first obsolete. But whatever is becoming obsolete and growing old is ready to disappear" (Heb 8:13; cp. Matt 24:1–2; John 4:21). He must be looking through the literal temple in Jerusalem to something more glorious. But what?

In the New Testament the *church* is spoken of as being God's house or temple. For instance, Paul speaks of the church as a "building, being fitted together . . . and growing into a holy temple in the Lord" (Eph 2:19). Several other references speak similarly (1 Cor 3:16; 6:19; 2 Cor 6:16; 1 Pet 2:5).

According to Isaiah, then, the "house of the LORD," which is the church, will be exalted during the course of the last days. This should not surprise us since Jesus says that his people are to be like a city set on a hill to influence the world (Matt 5:14; Heb 12:22; Rev 14:1; 21:10). And that his kingdom will grow to be a great plant in the world (Matt 13:31–32) and like leaven that penetrates all (Matt 13:31). And that he "will draw all men to Myself" (John 12:32). Thus, he commands us to "make disciples of all the nations" (Matt 28:19).

According to the New Testament the church is the focal point (though *not* the totality) of Christ's kingdom. When Jesus promises Peter "I will build my church" (Matt 16:18), he immediately says to him: "I will give you the keys of the *kingdom of heaven*" (Matt 16:19).

"It will be established." As we continue in Isaiah's prophecy we learn that "house of the LORD" (Christ's church) will be "established" in "the top of the mountains" (Isa 2:2c). The Hebrew word translated "established" is *kun*, which indicates something "permanently fixed, rendered permanently visible."[4]

Significantly, in the Hebrew Isaiah places the word "established" immediately after the introductory phrase "last days." This word order emphasizes the fact that it is "established." Literally, the translation reads: "in the last days, established will be the mountain." In the Old Testament eschatological portrayals of God's house, it appears as gigantic (Eze 40:2,

---

[4] J. A. Alexander, *Commentary on the Prophecies of Isaiah* (Grand Rapids: Zondervan, 1977 [rep. 1977]), 1:97.

5) and therefore quite secure. Indeed, Jerusalem wherein the Lord's house resides will expand her borders (Isa 54:1–5) and tower over a plain (Zech 14:10). Thus, the church is so firmly established as to tower over the world.

Jesus teaches that the church is so secure a fixture in the earth that the "gates of hell" cannot prevail against her (Matt 16:18). Hebrews informs us that she may not "be shaken": "we receive a kingdom which cannot be shaken" (Heb 12:28). Thus, in both Isaiah 2:2 and Micah 4:1 the result "must be understood of an enduring condition."[5]

"All the nations will stream to it." The exaltation of the Lord's house is such that "all the nations will stream" (Isa 2:2d) into the church. Political force does not compel them; no battle of Armageddon will cause this mass movement. Rather, the grace of God motivates them to enter into God's kingdom. For they will freely say: "Come, let us go up to the mountain of the LORD, / To the house of the God of Jacob" (Isa 2:3b-c).

As previously noted, this is precisely what Christ himself expects. As he approaches the time of his death, he promises: "I, if I am lifted up from the earth, will draw all men to Myself" (John 12:32). Indeed, this is the very reason he came into the world: "God did not send the Son into the world to judge the world, but that the world might be saved through Him" (John 3:17).

"That he may teach us concerning His ways." The nations will gladly stream to the Lord's house in order that "He may teach us concerning His ways" (Isa 2:3d). Here is pictured Christianity's gracious redemptive influence in the world. The swelling river of people will urge others to "come, let us go up" to the house of God (Isa 2:3a), which portrays successful evangelism leading to instruction in the things of God so that "we may walk in His paths" (Isa 2:3e).

Once again, this is what Jesus himself commands his people to secure: "Go therefore and make disciples of all the nations, baptizing them in the name of the Father and the Son and the Holy Spirit, teaching them to observe all that I commanded you; and lo, I am with you always, even to the end of the age" (Matt 28:19–20).

"Zion and Jerusalem." Now we must note that Isaiah mentions Zion and Jerusalem (Isa 2:3f, g). Isaiah parallels "Zion" and "Jerusalem" as meaning the same thing. This functions like the parallels throughout the

---

[5] Geerhardus Vos, *The Pauline Eschatology* (Phillipsburg, N.J.: Presbyterian and Reformed, rep. 1991 [1930]), 7.

prophecy: "chief of the mountains"="above the hills"; "all nations"= "many peoples"; "His ways=His paths"; and so forth. This Zion/Jerusalem image reflects the church in the new covenant era.

The New Testament speaks of people as coming to Zion and Jerusalem when they are converted: "you have come to Mount Zion and to the city of the living God, the heavenly Jerusalem" (Heb 12:22). Paul states that the church is the earthly manifestation of the city of God, for he teaches the Galatians that "the Jerusalem above is free; she is our mother" (Gal 4:25–26; cp. 1 Pet 2:6; Rev 21:2).

This association of Jerusalem with the church is because historical Jerusalem is where Christ effected redemption (Acts 10:39; Rom 9:33; 1 Pet 2:6) and where Christianity began (Luke 24:47, 52; Acts 1:8; 2:1ff). The historical "city of peace" stands as a symbol of the trans-national, suprahistorical city of God from which the peace of God ultimately flows.

"He will render decisions for many peoples." With overwhelming numbers converting to Christ and being discipled in God's law and ways, great socio-political transformation naturally follows:

"He will judge between the nations, / And will render decisions for many peoples; / And they will hammer their swords into plowshares, and their spears into pruning hooks. / Nation will not lift up sword against nation, / And never again will they learn war" (Isa 2:4).

This is an image of universal peace that is caused by "the Prince of Peace" (Isa 9:6). This corresponds with the Psalmist's prayer: "In his days may the righteous flourish, / And abundance of peace till the moon is no more" (Psa 72:7).

So here in Isaiah's great prophecy, peace with God (Isa 2:2–3) results in peace among men (Isa 2:4). Here we learn that God's gracious adoption overcomes man's sinful alienation. We must remember that he expects this as the result of the church being exalted and many peoples flowing into it. This is the very goal of postmillennialism: universal righteousness and peace. Our Lord even taught us to pray to this end, for we are to pray: "thy kingdom come, thy will be done on earth as it is in heaven" (Matt 6:10).

Conclusion

As we have seen in our brief analysis of the Psalms and the Prophets, the Old Testament presents us with the optimistic prospect of the global victory of Christ's redemptive kingdom. Earlier in chapter 2 of our study we saw that the Old Testament lays the foundations for the postmillennial hope by opening with God's creating the earth for his glory (Gen 1:1), establishing man in it as his image, and calling him to exercise dominion over it (Gen 1:26–27). Immediately upon man's fall into sin, the Lord promises redemption in order to crush Satan in history (Gen 3:15). This redemptive hope is secured by covenant promises involving all the families of the earth (Gen 12:1–3).

Consequently, in our current chapter we should not be surprised to find many Messianic Psalms and kingdom prophecies anticipating a time of universal blessedness and dominion for God's people (Psa 22:27; Isa 2:2–4). The Old Testament powerfully anticipates the victory of Christ's universal kingdom:

"They will not hurt or destroy in all My holy mountain, / For the earth will be full of the knowledge of the LORD / As the waters cover the sea. / Then in that day / The nations will resort to the root of Jesse, / Who will stand as a signal for the peoples; / And His resting place will be glorious." (Isa 11:9–10)

REVIEW QUESTIONS FOR DISCUSSION

These questions deal directly with the material in this chapter. The answers can be found in the chapter.

1. Though the Psalms were written for Israel's use (and mostly for her worship), they often make a universal point. Cite some Psalm verses that feed the postmillennial hope for the worldwide conquest of the gospel.
2. What appears to be the most important Psalm for the New Testament church? Why would we say this? What does it teach?
3. Throughout Scripture we see fallen man struggling against God, as anticipated in Genesis 3:15. Psalm 2 pictures that struggle. What elements in this psalm demonstrate that man's resistance to God is futile?
4. Why should we not interpret the reference to being "begotten" in Psalm 2:7 of Christ's birth? to what does it refer? Provide evidence.
5. In what way may we see the influence of Psalm on the Lord's Great Commission? Explain.
6. The great Christmas prophecy in Isaiah 9:6–7 speaks of Christ's accepting governmental rule. How should we understand his taking the

government on his shoulders? What in the passage suggests a postmillennial outlook?
7. Isaiah 2:2 sets its time of prophetic fulfilment as occurring "in the last days." When do the last days occur? What is the significance of this time frame to the postmillennial argument?
8. When Isaiah 2:2–3 mentions "the house of the Lord," "Zion," and "Jerusalem," to what is it referring? Provide biblical evidence to support your answer.
9. Note and elaborate on the points of contact exist between Isaiah 2:2–4 and the Lord's great commission in Matthew 28:18–20.
10. Which elements in the Isaiah 2:2–4 prophecy underscore the postmillennial hope for the future?

STRETCHING FURTHER

1. Other than Isaiah 2, which of the prophecies listed in this chapter do you see as the most significant for the postmillennial hope? Why?
2. Postmillennialism, like all eschatological systems, are not erected on just a few, select verses. Though key passages are foundational to any system, they are only a sampling of the many available texts. Can you cite some other references from the Psalms or Prophets in the Old Testament which encourage postmillennial expectations?
3. Obviously, adherents to the other millennial positions have their own, differing interpretations of the prophecies cited in this chapter. How would the other positions explain the prophecies that postmillennialists use for encouraging a gradualistic, historical unfolding of the kingdom in history?
4. Why might Isaiah's prophecies be particularly significant for early Christian understanding as well as our today?
5. What were some new ideas you learned from this chapter?

Chapter 4
POSTMILLENNIALISM IN THE GOSPELS

The entire Old Testament — its genealogies, revelation, prophecies, typology, and sacrificial system — anticipates and prepares for the coming of Christ in the first century. According to Jeremiah 31:31–34 the old covenant speaks of the new covenant which will take the place of and excel the old covenant. The writer of Hebrews agrees, arguing in Hebrews 8:7–13 that the old covenant is fading away and about to end because of the coming of the greater new covenant (cp. 2 Cor 3:7–13)

In the New Testament the Lord Jesus Christ expressly fulfills the Old Testament hope. For instance, in John 5:39 he declares to the religious authorities in Israel (here called "the Jews," John 5:15): "You search the Scriptures because you think that in them you have eternal life; it is these that testify about Me." He especially fulfills the prophecy regarding the Messiah, the long-expected Davidic king. In his public ministry he presents himself as the king who has come to establish his kingdom in order to establish his universal rule. The Gospel writers present him as king.

The Anticipation of the King

Shortly after Luke's Gospel opens, the angel Gabriel announces to Mary that she is pregnant (Luke 1:31, 34). He informs her that God will give to her son the throne of David:

"He will be great, and will be called the Son of the Most High; and the Lord God will give Him the throne of His father David; and He will reign over the house of Jacob forever; and His kingdom will have no end" (vv 32–33).

Upon learning of this news Mary goes to visit her relative Elizabeth (Luke 1:36, 39–40). When Elizabeth declares her blessed (vv 42, 45), Mary breaks into praise for God's goodness. By prophetic impulse she proclaims the kingdom-victory theme promised in the Old Testament. She declares that through her son, God will do "mighty deeds with His arm" for he will "scatter those who were proud" (v 51). The postmillennial hope is reverberating in the announcement of Jesus' coming birth.

Mary speaks with a prophetic past tense — as if the prophecy had already occurred, thereby emphasizing its certainty. She exults that God "has brought down rulers from their thrones, / And has exalted those who were humble" (Luke 1:52). She continues by praising God who "has filled the hungry with good things" (v 53) and "has given help to Israel" (v 54) in keeping with the Abrahamic Covenant: "As He spoke to our fathers, / To Abraham and his offspring forever" (v 55). All of this is in keeping with the postmillennial victory theme.

When Elizabeth's son (John the Baptist) is born a few months prior to Jesus (Luke 1:36, 57), her husband Zacharias also praises God with great joy. Through prophetic inspiration (v 67) Zacharias recognizes that his son John will be God's prophet and the forerunner of Jesus the Messiah (v 76). His own prophecy speaks of God's redemptive work in Christ as effecting victory over the enemy (vv 68–69, 71) through fulfillment of Old Testament prophecy (v 70) and the Abrahamic Covenant (vv 73; cp. Rom 15:8–12). This continues echoing a hope-filled optimism, securing for us the postmillennial hope.

Summarizing all of this, we learn that Jesus was born to be the king who will sit on David's throne to rule over God's people. By his coming God is scattering proud sinners who oppose his people. The result will be that he will bring down evil rulers and help God's people in keeping the Abrahamic Covenant. He will accomplish redemption and bring deliverance from their enemies.

The Approaching of the Kingdom

In the Gospels we discover Christ being introduced to Israel and the world through the ministry of John Baptist (Luke 1:76). John himself even fulfills prophecy by being the Messiah's forerunner (Isa 40:3; Matt 3:3). He prepares the way for Jesus by preaching: "Repent, for the kingdom of heaven is at hand" (Matt 3:2). And Jesus picks up on this theme as he begins his own ministry in Mark 1:14–15:

> "And after John had been taken into custody, Jesus came into Galilee, preaching the gospel of God, and saying, 'The time is fulfilled, and the kingdom of God is at hand; repent and believe the gospel.'"

Let's consider three crucial factors flowing out of this important pronouncement

First, Jesus declares "the time" has arrived. What is "the time" to which he refers? It surely speaks of the prophetically-anticipated time, the time of the coming of David's greater Son to establish his kingdom. We may surmise this in that he immediately adds: "the *kingdom of God* is at hand." After all, the Father sent Christ into the world in "the fullness of time" (Gal 4:4; Eph 1:10), to initiate the "favorable year of the Lord" (Luke 4:16–21). This favorable year of the Lord is also called "the acceptable time . . . the day of salvation" (2 Cor 6:2). It is the very day righteous men and angels in the old covenant long desired to see (Matt 13:17; Luke 2:28–30; 10:24; John 8:56; Heb 11:13, 39–40; 2 Pet 1:10–11).

Second, Jesus proclaims that the time "is fulfilled." He does not say "the time *may* be fulfilled — *if* you will receive the promise." Or: "the time *will* be fulfilled at some unknown date in the future." Rather he forthrightly declares that the God-ordained time *is* fulfilled now. Because of this Paul can later call this "the now time" (2 Cor 6:2; cf. Rom 3:21–26; Eph 3:10; 2 Tim 1:9–10). Though John and Jesus announce that the time is fulfilled, Jerusalem did not recognize the coming of "the time" (Luke 19:44; cf. Matt 23:37).

Third, "the kingdom of God is at hand." Since "the time" has arrived, and since it is "fulfilled," the kingdom of God is finally close, being right at hand. The coming of the kingdom does not await the distantly future return of Christ. Rather, during his *first* coming, at the very opening of his ministry, Jesus preaches that "the kingdom of God is at hand."

All of this is crucial to our eschatological understanding — and in keeping with postmillennial expectations. The kingdom's early new covenant revelation declares its *nearness* in time, not its potential nearness, and certainly not its distance. As a result of this glorious reality, Jesus promises that some of his hearers would live to see the kingdom's acting in *great power* in history: "There are some of those who are standing here who shall not taste of death until they see the kingdom of God after it has come *with power*" (Mark 9:1).

Thus, not only is his kingdom present in his ministry, but some of his disciples will actually live to see its exhibition *in power*. This exhibition would not be immediately, for some of his disciples would die first. Yet this must occur within the lifetimes of others, for "some" standing there would witness it.

The announcement in Mark 9:1 apparently refers to the dramatic AD 70 destruction of the temple and the removal of the Old Testament worship system. The writer of Hebrews anticipates the old covenant's conclusion: "When He said, 'A new covenant,' He has made the first obsolete. But whatever is becoming obsolete and growing old is ready to disappear" (cf. Heb 8:13; 12:25–28). This occurs as a direct result of Jesus' prophecies of the altering of divine worship (John 4:21–23) that results from the destruction of the temple (Matt 21:33–46; 22:1–7; 23:31–24:34).

The Establishing of the Kingdom

Jesus opens his ministry with the declaration that "the time" is "fulfilled" and the "kingdom of God" is "at hand." Thus, we should expect the kingdom to appear in Jesus' ministry and in the Gospel record. This is precisely what we discover in the Gospels.

Perhaps one of the clearest Gospel proofs of the presence of the kingdom is Matthew 12:28: "if I cast out demons by the Spirit of God, then the kingdom of God is come unto you." Since Jesus *does* cast out demons by the Spirit of God, *then* the kingdom *has come*. The very fact that Christ invades Satan's kingdom and takes away possessions (demoniacs, Matt 12:25–29) proves that the kingdom comes during his ministry.

Luke records for us another announcement of the kingdom's presence in Luke 17:20–21:

"Now having been questioned by the Pharisees as to when the kingdom of God was coming, He answered them and said, 'The kingdom of God is not coming with signs to be observed; nor will they say, "Look, here it is!" or, "There it is!" For behold, the kingdom of God is in your midst.'"

Notice that Christ answers the Pharisees' specific question regarding "when" the kingdom should come. He answers them in the present tense, informing them that the kingdom *is* present now. It is not awaiting a future, visible, Armageddon-introduced manifestation, complete with signs; it exists spiritually now and among them.

Because of this, even during his ministry men enter into it: "The Law and the Prophets were proclaimed until John; since then the gospel of the kingdom of God is preached, and everyone is forcing his way into it" (Luke 16:16). Christ's kingdom is not awaiting some distant future coming.

During his trial under Pilate, the Lord speaks directly of his kingship and kingdom:

"Jesus answered, 'My kingdom is not of this world. If My kingdom were of this world, then My servants would be fighting, that I might not be delivered up to the Jews; but as it is, My kingdom is not of this realm.' Pilate therefore said to Him, 'So You are a king?' Jesus answered, 'You say correctly that I am a king. For this I have been born, and for this I have come into the world, to bear witness to the truth.'" (John 18:36 –37a; see also: Matt 27:11; Mark 15:2; Luke 23:3)

Here Jesus defines his kingdom as something other-worldly, rather than as a this-worldly political kingdom. His kingdom differs from Caesar's political kingdom — and it differs from the dispensationalist's political conception of the Messianic kingdom. He claims to have his own "servants" (even though they do not fight with sword to defend Him, John 18:36b). He even clearly states "I am a king" (John 18:37a). And, as we might expect, given our study of Mark 1:14–15, he states that he has come into the world for the purpose of being king (John 18:37c). Thus, his kingdom is already present for we read of Jesus' affirmation that he is a king: "You say correctly that I am a king" (John 18:37a).

In all of this we see Christ himself stating that he was establishing his Messianic kingdom during his earthly ministry in his first coming. This is precisely the position of postmillennialism, though this contradicts the position of dispensationalism.

The Advancing of the Kingdom

Jesus presents his kingdom through his teaching and his practice, his words and his actions. He especially describes his kingdom in his Kingdom Parables, one of his major recorded discourses (Matt 13:1–52). Here he speaks in parables so that his followers might "know the *mysteries* of the kingdom of heaven" (Matt 13:11). These parables explain the mystery character of the kingdom, highlighting its hidden nature, small presence, and wavering condition (Matt 13:9–17, 19–22, 35–28, 31, 33, 44–45).

The Lord does not present a kingdom such as the first-century Jews and current-day dispensationalists expect. He does not lead a catastrophically-imposed, immediately-victorious, globally-dominating, military-political kingdom. Rather, he teaches something radically different. In fact, even his followers (who held first-century Jewish expectations) are initially confused about his kingdom: they "were hoping that it was He who was going to redeem Israel" (Luke 24:21; cp. Matt 13:36).

As per the postmillennial system the Kingdom Parables sketch the *present, spiritual, developmental*, and *dominating* nature of the kingdom. The present, spiritual, developmental nature of the kingdom contradicts the first-century Zionistic and current-century dispensationalist conceptions. The dominating nature of the kingdom clashes with the amillennial scheme. Let us consider three of the seven Kingdom Parables to mold our understanding.

The Parable of the Sower

In his first parable (Matt 13:3–23) we find material that fits well within a postmillennial scheme and differs greatly from dispensationalist and premillennialist expectations. This parable underscores Christ's rejection of any political and militaristic conceptions of his kingdom. We see his resistance to such a view in another context when he perceives that a crowd was "intending to come and take Him by force, to make Him king," for he "withdrew again to the mountain by Himself alone" (John 6:15).

In this parable Jesus notes that the kingdom which he proclaims spreads by means of God's Word (cp. Matt 26:51–52; Luke 17:30–31) — not by "sword's loud clashing." And that its message fails to convert some hearers (Matt 13:18–23) — it will not dramatically win the victory all at once. He even explains that Satan hampers the kingdom's growth (Matt 13:19). But despite all of this, the kingdom nevertheless gradually "bears fruit, and brings forth, some a hundredfold, some sixty, and some thirty" in those who convert (Matt 13:23). Furthermore, in the first century Christ sows his kingdom in the world in seed form — rather than presenting it as a full-blown kingdom coming dramatically at some distantly future date.

The Parable of the Mustard Seed

In the parable of the mustard seed, Christ teaches that: "The kingdom of heaven is like a mustard seed, which a man took and sowed in his field, which indeed is the least of all the seeds; but when it is grown it is greater than the herbs and becomes a tree, so that the birds of the air come and nest in its branches" (Matt 13:31–32).

All would agree that this image symbolizes something magnificent beyond expectation: a minuscule mustard seed grows to become a large tree. Though birds could easily eat a mustard seed, the mature mustard plant becomes large enough that they flock to it in order to build their nests for their young.

The Lord seems to build this parable by adapting imagery suggested by Ezekiel's kingdom prophecy in Ezekiel 17:22–24:

> "I will also take of the highest branch of the high cedar, and will set it; I will crop off from the top of his young twigs a tender one, and will plant it upon an high mountain. In the mountain of the height of Israel will I plant it: and it shall bring forth boughs, and bear fruit, and be a goodly cedar: and under it shall dwell all fowl of every wing; in the shadow of the branches thereof shall they

dwell. And all the trees of the field shall know that I the Lord have brought down the high tree, have exalted the low tree."

Here Ezekiel is symbolizing the universal magnificence and exaltation of the kingdom of heaven by contrasting it to Babylon's kingdom (Eze 17:14). God's kingdom will graciously provide shelter for all when it comes to full fruition in history. Both Ezekiel's prophecy and Jesus' parable point to the promised dominance of the heavenly kingdom in history: the small twig is planted on a high mountain above all the trees allows birds to nest in its branches; the tiny mustard seed is planted and becomes the largest plant in the garden allowing birds to nest in its branches.

So then, the Mustard Seed Parable speaks of the kingdom's massive, gradualistic *extension* in the world (cp. Matt 13:37–38). Clearly the kingdom will grow to a *large* size *over time*. It will not remain insignificantly small, nor will it erupt on the historical scene by catastrophic imposition. This fits the Old Testament expectation that he will "rule from sea to sea / And from the River to the ends of the earth" (Psa 72:8).

The Parable of the Leaven

The Lord's next parable employs leaven as the key symbol. It reads: "The kingdom of heaven is like leaven, which a woman took and hid in three measures of meal till it was all leavened" (Matt 13:33).

Here Christ symbolizes the kingdom's *intensive* progress in the world. Leaven is a *penetrative* agent that incrementally *diffuses itself* throughout its host from within (cf. Luke 17:20–21), for "a little leaven leavens the whole lump of dough" (1 Cor 5:6; Gal 5:9).

Thus, here the leaven will thoroughly penetrate the whole three pecks of meal (which represents "the world," as in Matt 13:38). The kingdom will *penetrate all* (Matt 13:33). This was implied in other Kingdom Parables: the kingdom will produce a *hundred-fold* return in its converts (Matt 13:8). It will *dominate* the field (world*)* (Matt 13:30). It will grow to *great stature* (Matt 13:31–32).

The Kingdom Parables' theme

Both the Parable of the Mustard Seed and the Parable of the Leaven present Christ's kingdom as gradually developing in history by the process of *growth*. Clearly Christ here explains the progressive *nature* and global *extent* of the kingdom that he is establishing during his ministry. After all, he opens his ministry by proclaiming "the kingdom of heaven is at hand" (Matt 4:17; cp. 3:2; 10:7). Then he immediately sets out preaching that kingdom (Matt 4:23) as a present reality (Matt 5:3, 10, 19; 6:33; 9:35; 12:28), which begins in earnest in the days of John the Baptist (Matt 11:11–12).

The kingdom of Christ does *not* come catastrophically as a full-blown, world-dominating kingdom; rather it comes gradually as it grows toward worldwide victory. This gradualism contradicts the premillennial view. Its dominance contradicts the amillennial position.

The Commissioning by the King

As a king ruling over a kingdom destined to grow, the Lord directs his servants to promote that growth. And as their sovereign, he not only commands their labor but promises his presence with them to accomplish his goal. He is a king with a mission.

Christ's post-resurrection, pre-ascension Great Commission clearly declares his enthronement and his mission to world conquest. We must hear and follow the sovereign declaration of the risen Lord:

> "And Jesus came up and spoke to them, saying, 'All authority has been given to Me in heaven and on earth. Go therefore and make disciples of all the nations, baptizing them in the name of the Father and the Son and the Holy Spirit, teaching them to observe all that I commanded you; and lo, I am with you always, even to the end of the age.'" (Matt 28:18–20)

Let's closely consider the Great Commission in terms of its significance as a foundation stone of postmillennialism.

The King's authority

Christ prefaces the actual commission with a bold — and essential — claim: "All authority has been given to Me in heaven and on earth." The word "given" is significant for both its position in the sentence and its tense. "Given" appears in the first position for emphasis and is a past tense declaration. But how is this significant?

Obviously the past point in time when this occurs is at Jesus' resurrection from the dead. The historical circumstances of the Great Commission suggest this, for Christ utters the Commission shortly after his resurrection (cf. Matt 28:1–10, 16). But other passages confirm this understanding. Let's note just two statements from Paul's writings.

- Romans 1:4: "was *declared* the Son of God with power *by* the resurrection from the dead."

- Philippians 2:8, 9: "He humbled Himself by becoming obedient to the point of death, even death on a cross. Therefore also God exalted Him, and *bestowed* on Him the name which is above every name."

Thus, at his resurrection Christ steps out of his state of humiliation and suffering to his estate of exaltation and glory. Whereas previously he spoke only in submission to the Father (John 5:19, 30; 6:38; 8:28; 12:49; 14:10, 24), now he speaks with final authority due to his completed work.

As noted in the preceding chapter, this grant of kingly authority fulfills Psalm 2:6–7. The resurrection establishes Christ as the King possessing "all authority" — in the first century.

Matthew 28:18 indicates that something new occurs at his resurrection. He is *now* given "all authority" to go along with his kingship. The spoils of victory are his — victory over depravity, death, and the devil belong to him (Col 2:14, 15; Heb 2:13, 14; 10:12–14). His newfound authority entails *universal* dominion for it encompasses "heaven and earth." Thus, his authority is identical with God the Father's who possesses unbounded lordship: God is "Lord of heaven and earth" (Matt 11:25; cp. Gen 14:19, 22; Ezra 5:11; Luke 10:21; Acts 17:24).

Not only is Christ's authority *above* all other, but it *penetrates* every realm. It is not just in the spiritual arena (the inner-personal realm), but in all spheres of life. It universally and comprehensively serves as the basis for a truly Christian worldview. Let us see how this is so.

The "all" which defines "authority" is here used in the *distributive* sense, entailing every form of authority. That is, each and every realm of thought and activity is under his authoritative command: ecclesial, familial, and personal — as well as ethical, social, cultural, financial, judicial, legal, political, and every other realm. The rich reward of his redemptive labor is sovereign lordship over all (Eph 1:19–23; Col 1:18; Phil 2:9–10; 1 Pet 3:21–22; Rev 1:5; 17:14; 19:16).

The King's command

On the basis of this universal authority Christ commissions his disciples to "go therefore and make disciples of *all the nations*" (Matt 28:19a). This fits perfectly with his world-encompassing authority. The ascended Christ mandates that his Church promote and expand his kingdom in the world. Would he assert his sovereign lordship so vigorously and command his people so majestically were it not his intention that they fulfill his obligation?

We must recognize what the Great Commission actually commands. It does *not* send forth his disciples merely to "witness" or "proclaim" or "preach" the gospel (though all of these activities are involved).

According to the Commission's clear wording Christ commands his disciples actually to "make disciples of all the nations." That is, they must actually bring the nations under his discipleship yoke, by bringing them to salvation and baptizing them "in the name of the Father and the Son and the Holy Spirit." This is in keeping with his declaration elsewhere: "Now is the judgment of this world; now the ruler of this world will be cast out. And I, if I am lifted up from the earth, will draw all men to Myself" (John 12:31–32).

The King's promise

What is more, not only does he authoritatively command them to disciple all the nations on the basis of his redemptively-won, universal authority, but he even promises them that he will be with them (and all his people) "throughout all [literally] the days" (Matt 28:20). That is, he will be with them through the many days until the end to oversee the successful completing of the task.

This allows for the gradual development of his kingdom program through time. All nations will be discipled before the end comes. This is the postmillennial hope.

The Proclaiming of the Kingdom

The Gospels fit perfectly in the coherent message of Scripture that begins in creation, develops through covenant, and is promised victory in the Psalms and Prophets. And all that we learn in the Gospels undergirds what we hear so frequently in the remainder of the New Testament: the proclamation of the "kingdom of God."[1] In Acts 3:15 Peter preaches Christ as the "prince of life." In Acts 5:29 he asserts his obligation to disobey civil authority when it demands that he cease preaching Christ. His rationale is important: "He is the one whom God exalted to His right hand as a Prince and a Savior" (Acts 5:31). The word "prince" here may literally be translated "leader, ruler, prince." He is exalted as prince or ruler.

---

[1] See: Acts 8:12; 14:22; 19:8; 20:25; 28:23, 31; Rom 14:17; 1 Cor 4:20; 6:9–10; 15:50; Gal 5:21; Eph 5:5; Col 1:13; 4:11; 1 Thess 2:12; 2 Thess 1:5; 2Ti 4:1; 4:18; Heb 1:8; 12:28; Jms 2:5; 2 Pet 1:11.

That Christ has already become a king is evident in Acts 17:7. There non-believers attack the earliest Christians for proclaiming Christ as king. Just as the Jews accuse Jesus of claiming to be a king,[2] so we read of the charge against his followers: "These all do contrary to the decrees of Caesar, saying that there is another king, one Jesus." Just as Jesus declares himself a king, so his followers do the same. Though their assailants distort the implications of their preaching Christ's kingship, the fact remains: the early Christians *did* preach Christ as king.

Paul claims of Christ that God "put *all* things under his feet" (Eph 1:22; 1 Cor 15:27). This includes even political rule over the nations, for God "highly exalted Him, and bestowed on Him the name which is above *every name*, that at the name of Jesus *every knee* should bow, of those who are in heaven, and on earth, and under the earth" (Phil 2:9–10).

This explains the scores of references to him as "Lord" throughout the New Testament. His full title as preached in the New Testament is: "Lord Jesus Christ."[3] In fact, "Christ is Lord" evidently becomes a creedal statement of sorts in the apostolic era.[4]

Paul speaks to the Colossians about the kingdom: "giving thanks to the Father, who has qualified us to share in the inheritance of the saints in light. For He delivered us from the domain of darkness, and transferred us to the kingdom of His beloved Son" (Col 1:12, 13). He clearly considers this transferring of the Colossian Christians to the kingdom as a *past* act (nearly 2,000 years ago now), *not* a future prospect. Paul uses aorist (past) tense verbs when he speaks of their being "delivered" and "transferred"; he does the same in 1 Thessalonians 2:12. He also speaks of his ministry "for the kingdom of God" (Col 4:11).

John follows suit in Revelation 1:6 and 9, declaring God "has made us to be a kingdom, priests to His God and Father" and noting "I, John, your

---

[2] See: Matt 27:29, 37; Mark 15:12, 26; Luke 23:3; 24:21; John 18:33; 19:12, 15, 21.

[3] See: Acts 11:17; 15:25; 20:21; 28:31; Rom 1:7; 5:1, 11; 13:14; 15:6, 30; 16:24; 1 Cor 1:2–3, 7–8, 10; 6:11; 8:6:15:57; 2 Cor 1:2–3; 8:9; 13:14; Gal 1:3; 6:14, 18; Eph 1:2–3, 17; 5:20; 6:23–24; Phil 1:2; 3:20; 4:23; Col 1:3; 1 Thess 1:1, 3; 5:9, 23, 28; 2 Thess 1:1–2, 12–2:1, 2:14, 16; 26, 12, 18; 1 Tim 6:3, 14; Phile 1:3, 24; Jms 1:1; 2:1; 1 Pet 1:3, 8, 14, 16; Jude 4, 17, 21.

[4] Rom 10:9; 1Cor 12:3; Phil 2:11. See discussion of the creed-like status of this declaration in: Kenneth L. Gentry, Jr., *Nourishment from the Word* (Lincoln, Calif: Nordskog, 2008), 4–6.

brother and fellow partaker in the tribulation and kingdom and perseverance which are in Jesus." In these verses John speaks of first-century Christians (Rev 1:4, 11; 2–3) as already "made" (aorist tense) to be "a kingdom" (literally). In fact, John is *already* a fellow with them in the "kingdom" (Rev 1:9).

Conclusion

As we continue our study of biblical eschatology, we have discovered in this chapter that we continue to detect the vibrant optimism of the eschatological hope of Scripture. It flows out of the Old Testament and begins making its life-giving presence felt in the New Testament experience. When Christ appears on the scene he declares: "The time is fulfilled, and the kingdom of God is at hand; repent and believe in the gospel" (Mark 1:15). Later in his ministry he asserts his authority, announcing: "If I cast out demons by the Spirit of God, then the kingdom of God has come upon you" (Matt 12:28). His kingdom is not to wait thousands of years; he comes as King in the first century.

Christ's coming not only establishes the kingdom but initiates its growth to victory through time, as it dynamically grows like a mustard seed to a great planet dominating the garden (Matt 13:31–32). Its growth is secured by God's grant of "all authority" to Christ and his commissioning of his disciples to "make disciples of all the nations" (Matt 28:20). Truly, Jesus is Lord and rules over his conquering kingdom now.

REVIEW QUESTIONS FOR DISCUSSION

These questions deal directly with the material in this chapter. The answers can be found in the chapter.

1. At what stage in New Testament history do the Gospels begin to speak of Christ's coming to be a king?
2. Recalling the significance of the Abrahamic Covenant (as we learned in chapter 2), what role does the Abrahamic Covenant play in Jesus' birth narratives?
3. At the very beginning of his public ministry, Jesus makes an important statement regarding the Messianic kingdom. What are the key features of his statement that support a postmillennial conception and contradict a dispensational one?

4. How do Jesus' Kingdom Parables present his kingdom? How does this scheme differ from dispensationalism's view of the kingdom and its coming?
5. What event must occur before Christ can issue his great commission? Why?
6. With what words does the great commission open? How are these significant for allowing for the postmillennial hope? That is, what do they imply?
7. What does the great commission expect in history? What is the role of the church in this expectation?
8. What elements in the great commission should encourage us to confidently promote the Christian faith throughout the world?
9. What do Acts' history and its record of the Apostolic preaching suggest about the coming of the kingdom? Cite verses to support your answer and discuss their implications.
10. Based on several verses employed in this chapter, does the Christian faith have political implications? That is, does it suggest any Christian interest in and involvement in civil governmental affairs?

STRETCHING FURTHER

1. Can you list some Christian hymns that present a postmillennial viewpoint?
2. A favorite hymn of many Christians is "There Is None Like the Lowly Jesus." Explain why this hymn either is or is not proper to sing today.
3. How is Hebrews 8:13 (in its whole context) important as a rebuttal to dispensationalism (see chapter 1 for the descriptive features of dispensationalism).
4. The Gospels speak of "the kingdom of God" and "the kingdom of heaven." Are they referring to different realities? How do you know?
5. What were some new ideas you learned from this chapter?

Chapter 5
POSTMILLENNIALISM IN PAUL

In the New Testament the temporary old covenant fades as the permanent new covenant is established. Christ is the founder and Lord of the new covenant phase (Luke 22:20; 1 Cor 11:25) of the church (Matt 16:18; Eph 1:22; 5:23). Consequently, we expect that his Apostles and other New Testament writers will continue proclaiming the victory theme which he began during his earthly ministry. And they certainly do.

Space limitations prohibit a comprehensive, in-depth analysis of this glorious truth in the remainder of the New Testament.[1] But such is not needed, for in Paul — the writer of thirteen of the New Testament's twenty-seven books and the great systematic theologian of the Apostles — we find a compelling and bold advocate of Christ's dominion in history. In this chapter we will focus on two leading passages in his writings.

Before we turn to those passages, though, we should recall that the Jesus appears personally to Saul (soon to be called "Paul," Acts 13:9), the great persecutor of the Church (Acts 8:3; 9:1–2; 22:4; 26:9–12; Gal 1:13–14; Phil 3:6). He not only saves Saul/Paul from his sins, but directly commissions him as a minister to God's people (Acts 9:3–22; 22:6–15; 26:12–18; Gal 1:15–16).

Because of Saul's notoriety as a persecutor of Christians, Ananias initially fears him. When Jesus appears to Ananias in a dream and calls him to go visit Saul, he recoils: "Lord, I have heard from many about this man, how much harm he did to Your saints at Jerusalem'" (Acts 9:13). But Jesus informs him about Saul's conversion and commission: "the Lord said to him, 'Go, for he is a chosen instrument of Mine, to bear My name before the Gentiles and kings and the sons of Israel'" (Acts 9:15).

Significantly for our purposes, Jesus commissions Paul soon after his conversion. Later Paul gives his testimony before King Agrippa, informing him that the Lord said to him: I am "delivering you from the Jewish people and from the Gentiles, to whom I am sending you, to open their eyes so that they may turn from darkness to light and from the dominion

---

[1] For more information, see my 600 page book: *He Shall Have Dominion: A Postmillennial Eschatology* (Draper, Vir.: ApologeticsGroup, 2009).

of Satan to God, in order that they may receive forgiveness of sins and an inheritance among those who have been sanctified by faith in Me" (Acts 26:17–18).

Paul accepts Christ's commission, testifying that the Lord informs him (on the basis of Scripture): "I have placed you as a light for the Gentiles, / That You should bring salvation to the end of the earth" (Acts 13:47). Thus, Paul "went about preaching the kingdom" (Acts 20:25; cp. Acts 19:8; 28:23, 31).

As a good servant of his Master, Christ, Paul also views the kingdom as does Christ: the kingdom he preached was a spiritual reality, rather than a political institution. In Romans 14:17 we read that the kingdom is "righteousness and peace and joy in the Holy Spirit." He informs those who have been converted to Christ that "no immoral or impure person or covetous man, who is an idolater, has an inheritance in the kingdom of Christ and God" (Eph 5:5).

We know that the kingdom is a spiritual reality entered into by believers beginning in the first century, for Paul clearly declares this. Notice how he uses the past tense in writing to the Colossians about their membership in God's kingdom: "He delivered us from the domain of darkness, and transferred us to the kingdom of His beloved Son" (Col 1:13).

So now let us see how Paul picks up on the Old Testament expectation and the Gospels' initiation of the universal triumph of the gospel. We see this best in two extensive passages that focus on eschatological themes: Romans 11:11–26 and 1 Corinthians 15:20–28.

Romans 11:11–26

In Romans 11 we discover an extremely important eschatological passage from Paul. And in the core of that passage, verses 11–26, we find much evidence for the postmillennial hope:

> "I say then, they [the Jews] did not stumble so as to fall, did they? May it never be! But by their transgression salvation has come to the Gentiles, to make them jealous. Now if their transgression be riches for the world and their failure be riches for the Gentiles, how much more will their fulfillment be! But I am speaking to you who are Gentiles. Inasmuch then as I am an apostle of Gentiles, I magnify my ministry, if somehow I might move to jealousy my fellow countrymen and save some of them. For if their rejection be the reconciliation of the world, what will

their acceptance be but life from the dead? And if the first piece of dough be holy, the lump is also; and if the root be holy, the branches are too. But if some of the branches were broken off, and you, being a wild olive, were grafted in among them and became partaker with them of the rich root of the olive tree, do not be arrogant toward the branches; but if you are arrogant, remember that it is not you who supports the root, but the root supports you. You will say then, 'Branches were broken off so that I might be grafted in.' Quite right, they were broken off for their unbelief, but you stand by your faith. Do not be conceited, but fear; for if God did not spare the natural branches, neither will He spare you. Behold then the kindness and severity of God; to those who fell, severity, but to you, God's kindness, if you continue in His kindness; otherwise you also will be cut off. And they also, if they do not continue in their unbelief, will be grafted in; for God is able to graft them in again. For if you were cut off from what is by nature a wild olive tree, and were grafted contrary to nature into a cultivated olive tree, how much more shall these who are the natural branches be grafted into their own olive tree?

"For I do not want you, brethren, to be uninformed of this mystery, lest you be wise in your own estimation, that a partial hardening has happened to Israel until the fulness of the Gentiles has come in; and thus all Israel will be saved; just as it is written, 'The Deliverer will come from Zion, / He will remove ungodliness from Jacob.'"

In Romans 11 Paul is focusing particularly on *ethnic* Jews, who were the special recipients of God's grace in the Old Testament (Rom 3:1–2; cp. Psa 147:19–20). He is teaching about their role in the new covenant phase of redemptive history. But, as in Israel's Psalms and Prophets, the way he handles the matter leads him to assert global optimism regarding Christianity's future — almost in passing as he simply *assumes* the gospel's global conquest. We should begin by noting the literary context of his argument.

Contextual flow

In Romans 8 and 9 Paul vigorously asserts God's absolute sovereignty.[2] But this causes a question to arise: What about the Jews? If God is sovereign, how can we explain their rejecting Christ and falling away from God's favor? Are they not "His people" (Rom 11:1, 2)? Were they not the adopted sons who possessed the promises of God (Rom 9:4)?

Romans 9–11 answers this important question regarding God's sovereignty in the light of Israel's rebellion. Paul is clearly dealing with ethnic Jews when he raises the question, for he writes: "I say then, God has not rejected His people, has He? May it never be! For I too am an Israelite, a descendant of Abraham, of the tribe of Benjamin" (Rom 11:1). He defines "His people" by referring to Israel's ethnic tribes (Rom 11:1), by citing Elijah's experience (Rom 11:2), and by distinguishing them from the Gentiles (Rom 11:11–13, 25).

As he engages the perplexing issue, he asks two questions: Has God rejected his people (Rom 11:1)? And has Israel stumbled for the purpose of absolutely falling away (Rom 11:11)? These are crucial questions for Paul's theology of the absolute sovereignty of God to resolve.

In answering these questions in his context, Paul argues that God's sovereignty does *not* fail because: First, even "at this present time there is a remnant according to the election of grace" (Rom 11:5; cp. 2–6) and God himself sovereignly hardens the rest (Rom 11:7–10). Second, God will bring the Jews back into God's favor in the future and on an equal footing with the saved Gentiles (Rom 11:11–26). Thus, the current presence of a remnant shows his rejection is not *total* and the future hope of their fullness shows that his rejection is not *final*.

Contextual point

The driving point of his analysis is stated in Romans 11:25–26a. The four basic millennial schools present distinctive approaches to Paul's statement, which reads: "For I do not want you, brethren, to be uninformed of this mystery, lest you be wise in your own estimation, that a partial hardening has happened to Israel until the fulness of the Gentiles has come in; and thus all Israel will be saved."

---

[2] For a full consideration of God's absolute sovereignty over all things, defending it against the charges that it is ethically immoral and intellectually absurd, see: Gentry, *Predestination Made Easy* (Draper, Vir.: ApologeticsGroup, 2010) ch. 7.

The premillennialist and the dispensationalist see the statement that "all Israel will be saved" as promising a future national, geo-political restoration of Israel's kingdom. Generally the amillennialist sees this as signifying that the Church fulfills Israel's promises by becoming the true Israel. The postmillennialist sees here the promise of world conversion as finally including ethnic Israel herself.

Postmillennial resolution

The postmillennial approach best fits the flow of Paul's argument. In the second phase of his argument proving that God's sovereignty does not fail, he explains that Israel did not stumble at Christ *for the purpose that* (Gk., *hina*) they might utterly and finally fall away (Rom 11:11). In *introducing* the problem he vigorously rejects any such prospect: "May it never be!" for "God has not rejected His people whom He foreknew" (Rom 11:1, 2).

He also rejects this possibility *immediately after posing the question*: "May it never be!" (Rom 11:11). Rather God's sovereign purpose in Israel's current condition is to bring in Gentile salvation, which will spark widespread Jewish conversions: "salvation has come to the Gentiles, to make them jealous" (Rom 11:11).

Paul then states: "Now if their transgression be riches for the world and their failure be riches for the Gentiles, how much more will their fulfillment be!" (Rom 11:12). We must understand that since Israel's loss is almost total (only a remnant remains, Rom 11:5), her "fulfillment" (Gk., *pleroma*) must be commensurate with her loss, which means it must be virtually total.

Hence, postmillennialists believe in future, massive conversions among the Jews, not only due to our general theological expectations regarding worldwide salvation, but also due to this particular exegetical evidence.

Amillennial objection

Amillennialists dismiss this view for two contextual reasons:

(1) This salvation of Israel is a "mystery" (Rom 11:25), which presents an unexpected resolution to the Jewish problem. That resolution is that the church becomes Israel so that God fulfills Israel's promises through her.

(2) In the opening phrase to Romans 11:26 Paul uses the phrase *kai houtos* ("and thus"), which means "in this manner," "in this way." This

phrase, so they argue, does not refer to temporal *sequence* tracing the falling away of the Jews, then the conversion of the Gentiles, followed finally by Israel's salvation. Rather it refers to the unexpected *manner* by which God fulfills his promise: by making the Gentile Church the fulfillment of Israel's hope.

Postmillennialism can answer both objections. First, in that Paul emphasizes ethnic Israel in his opening question (Rom 11:1–2) and in that he plays Gentiles over against Israel (Rom 11:11–13, 25), the "mystery" involved is the remarkable, unanticipated *method* God uses: he plays Israel off the Gentiles. This involves the salvific wave motion of Israel falling away from God's favor, Gentiles coming in, then Israel being drawn back in.

Second, regarding "and thus": though it is true that it often lacks sequential emphasis, this is not always the case. For instance, in 1 Corinthians 11:28 Paul writes: "But let a man examine himself, and so [same Greek phrase] let him eat of the bread and drink of the cup." Indeed, some major versions translate this usage temporally: "A man ought to examine himself *before* he eats of the bread and drinks of the cup" (NIV). "Examine yourselves, and only *then* eat of the bread and drink of the cup" (NRSV). Temporal sequence seems clear in other texts, as well (Acts 17: 33; 20:11; 1 Cor 14:25). This presents no problem to the postmillennial interpretation.

Consequently, in Romans 11 Paul speaks of Christianity's future glory: the Jewish failure will eventually bring "riches for the world" (Rom 11:12), resulting in "the reconciling of the world" (Rom 11:15), leading to "the fulness of the Gentiles" (Rom 11:25). All three references point to massive, worldwide conversions. All three underscore the postmillennial hope.

Another passage that powerfully presents an optimistic hope for world conversion is found it Paul's great resurrection chapter, to which we now turn.

1 Corinthians 15:20–28

Here in 1 Corinthians 15 Paul teaches not only that Christ *currently* sits upon the throne, but also that he rules with a confident view to *subduing his enemies* in history.

Be aware: in the discussion below we will be employing the New International Version as our basic English translation due to its greater fidelity to several particulars of the Greek grammar in this passage. The

Revised Standard Version and English Standard Version both provide a good rendering of the passage, as well

Paul writes in 1 Corinthians 15:20–28:

"But Christ has indeed been raised from the dead, the firstfruits of those who have fallen asleep. For since death came through a man, the resurrection of the dead comes also through a man. For as in Adam all die, so in Christ all will be made alive. But each in his own turn: Christ, the firstfruits; then, when he comes, those who belong to him. Then the end will come, when he hands over the kingdom to God the Father after he has destroyed all dominion, authority and power. For he must reign until he has put all his enemies under his feet. The last enemy to be destroyed is death. For he 'has put everything under his feet.' Now when it says that 'everything' has been put under him, it is clear that this does not include God himself, who put everything under Christ. When he has done this, then the Son himself will be made subject to him who put everything under him, so that God may be all in all."

The resurrection order

In 1 Corinthians 15:20–22 Paul speaks of the resurrection order: Christ is resurrected as a firstfruits promise of our own future resurrection. In verses 23–24 we read about the sequence of events involving the resurrection: "But each in his own turn: Christ the first fruits; then, when he comes, those who belong to him. Then the end will come." We today are currently in the era awaiting Christ's end-time coming, when all believers will arise in resurrection glory.

According to Paul, when Christ comes this will be "the end." Scripture is clear that the resurrection of believers occurs simultaneously with that of all men at the end of history. It teaches that there will be a "general resurrection" of both the righteous and unrighteous: "there shall certainly be a resurrection of both the righteous and the wicked" (Acts 24:15; John 5:28–29).

Scripture is equally clear that the resurrection will occur on the "last day": "this is the will of My Father, that everyone who beholds the Son and believes in Him will have eternal life, and I Myself will raise him up on the last day" (John 6:40; cp. John 6:39, 44, 54; 11:24; 12:48). Thus, according to Paul (and Jesus) no millennial age will follow. The resurrection of believers (and unbelievers) occurs on the "last day," not 1007[3] years before the "last day."

The eschatological victory

But notice what *precedes* the end. First Corinthians 15:24 says: "the end will come, when he hands over the kingdom to God the Father." Earth history ends "whenever"[4] Christ "hands over" the kingdom to the Father. In the Greek structure before us, his "handing over" (NIV) or "delivering up" (KJV) the kingdom occurs simultaneously with "the end." Here the timing is contingent: "whenever" he delivers up the kingdom, *then* the end will come. In addition, he will deliver up his kingdom to the Father only "*after* he has destroyed all dominion, authority and power."

So then, *the end of history is contingent:* it will come *whenever* it may be that Christ delivers up the kingdom to his Father. But this will not occur until "*after* He has destroyed all dominion, authority and power" (see also: RSV and ESV). Consequently, the end of history will not occur, and Christ will not turn the kingdom over to the Father, until *after* he has abolished *all* opposition. Here again we see the gospel victory motif in the New Testament in a way co-ordinate with Old Testament covenantal and prophetic expectations.

Notice further that Paul alludes to Psalm 110:1 at this juncture. 1 Corinthians 15:25 demands that "He *must* reign until He has put all His enemies under His feet." Here the present infinitive for "reign" indicates an *ongoing* reign that exists as Paul writes. The kingdom is present and Christ is ruling in the first century.

We saw in chapter 4 that Christ is presently reigning, and has been so since his ascension. References elsewhere to Psalm 110 specifically mention his sitting at God's right hand, which entails active ruling and reigning, not passive resignation or anxious waiting. As John informs us, Jesus is *now* "the ruler over the kings of the earth" and "has made us kings and priests to His God and Father, to Him be glory and dominion forever and ever" (Rev 1:5–6; cp. Rev 3:21).

---

[3] This would represent the seven-year great tribulation and the thousand year reign of Christ, both of which occur after the resurrection of believers in the dispensational system.

[4] A better translation of *hotan* is "whenever." We know not "when" this will be (Matt 24:36; Acts 1:7; 2 Pet 3:10).

Thus, in 1 Corinthians 11:25 Paul states that Christ must continue reigning as he puts his enemies under his feet. But to what point in time does his reign continue? The answer is identical to our previous conclusion: his reign from the right hand of God in heaven extends to the *end of history*.

We must understand his rule as definitive, progressive, and consummative. That is, during his earthly ministry he awaits his resurrection in order to secure the *definitive* (legal) right to all rule, authority and power (Matt 28:18; Eph 1:19–22; Phil 2:9–11; 1 Pet 3:21–22). Now that he rules from heaven until he returns, his return is delayed until he *progressively* (actively, continually, historically) puts "all His enemies under His feet" (Paul's repeating the fact of his sure conquest before the end is significant). Then *consummatively* (finally and fully), he will subdue our "last enemy," death, by means of the final resurrection at his coming.[5]

Thus, Christ's victory has a past, present, and future reality. Church history begins in the past with his *legal* victory at the cross-resurrection-ascension. It continues *progressively* in the present as he subdues all of his other enemies. Then it ends *finally* at the eschatological resurrection, which conquers the final enemy, death.

In 1 Corinthians 15:27 Christ clearly has the legal title to rule, for the Father "has put everything under His feet." This expression (borrowed from Psa 8:6) corresponds with Christ's declaring that "all authority has been given Me" (Matt 28:18). He has both the *right* to victory as well as the *promise* of victory. Psalm 110, especially as expounded by Paul in 1 Corinthians 15, shows that he will secure historical victory over all earthly opposition *before* his second advent — in time and on earth.

Conclusion

Paul is a faithful servant of Christ his Lord. He honors his Master by following his public instruction and pursuing his Great Commission. Despite the forces arrayed against him, he proclaims the total victory of Christ in history. He does not believe that God is snatching brands from the fire. Rather he firmly believes in the reconciliation of the whole world (Rom 11:15) and expects that Christ "must reign until He has put all His

---

[5] Contrary to dispensationalist confusion, the resurrection of the lost is not mentioned here only because his primary concern (as in 1 Thess 4:13) is with Christians and their ethical actions.

enemies under His feet" (1 Cor 15:25). His hope for history and the progress of the gospel feeds our postmillennial expectations.

REVIEW QUESTIONS FOR DISCUSSION

These questions deal directly with the material in this chapter. The answers can be found in the chapter.
1. How does Paul's calling by Christ impact the postmillennial outlook? Cite verses dealing with his call.
2. What verses in Paul suggest that Christ's kingdom is a present and spiritual reality rather than a future, governmental matter? Choose one of these and provide a brief discussion on its implications.
3. Romans 11 provides powerful evidence for the postmillennial hope. What is Paul's fundamental concern in Romans 9–11 which finally leads up to his eschatological statement?
4. List and briefly discuss the different millennial views' understanding of Romans 11:25–26. Highlight how they differ.
5. What is the key issue in the debate between the millennial schools in Romans 11? What is the postmillennial explanation of this matter?
6. Discuss the amillennialist objection to the postmillennial interpretation of this key issue. Explain the postmillennial response.
7. In 1 Corinthians 15:20–28 Paul is defending the future, literal resurrection of believers, which is an important eschatological issue. In his presentation he briefly outlines the order of the resurrection so that we may understand the relationship of Jesus' resurrection to our own. Discuss the significance of the order of events in terms of eschatological expectations.
8. What does Paul mean when he teaches that Jesus will "hand over" the kingdom to the Father? What is the significance of this regarding the timing, purpose, and conclusion of Christ's reign?
9. Explain the different senses (or theological phases) of Christ's kingly rule.
10. Discuss what Paul teaches must occur before he hands over the kingdom to the Father. Explain how this undergirds the postmillennial argument.

STRETCHING FURTHER

1. Liberal theologians argue that Paul amended Jesus' message, reducing its Jewish element in order to adapt it for a Gentile audience. How would a postmillennialist explain this apparent adaptation while defending Paul as a faithful representative of Christ?
2. Romans 11:25–26 is an important statement for eschatology. Discuss how these two verses require good theologians to look at the broader contexts of key verses and the narrative flow of their larger narrative settings for a proper interpretation.
3. Christians sometimes look back to the Apostolic church as the era of pristine, pure, focused Christianity. Discuss how both of our key Pauline passages show us that the earliest phase of Christianity was buffeted and troubled, requiring Apostolic correction of problems.
4. Discuss how passages dealing with ultimate, end time eschatology has a practical impact even on the first century church.
5. What were some new ideas you learned from this chapter?

Chapter 6
THE GREAT TRIBULATION IN POSTMILLENNIALISM

American evangelical Christians are intensely interested in what the New Testament calls "the great tribulation." Many enormously popular, best-selling books have been written on this phenomenon, including *The Late Great Planet Earth* (30 million copies sold) and the *Left Behind* series (65 million copies).

The great tribulation is significant and merits careful consideration. This is not only because of its influence on contemporary evangelical thought, but (more importantly) because of its large presence in Scripture. The Bible touches on this theme in many contexts in both the Old and New Testaments. Furthermore, it seems to contradict postmillennialism's historical optimism. Consequently, it will be crucial for us to study it in light of our presentation of the postmillennial hope.

Introduction

The two most significant portions of Scripture treating the great tribulation are found in Jesus' teaching and John's Revelation. It appears prominently in one of Christ's major recorded discourses: the Olivet Discourse in Matthew 24–25 (cp. Mark 13; Luke 21:5–36). The first thirty-four verses of Matthew 24 focus on the great tribulation, even employing the phrase in verse 21. The phrase also appears in the Book of Revelation (Rev 7:14), where the details of the great tribulation dominate virtually the entire book.

As pessimistic systems, the non-postmillennial eschatological positions see our future in the bleakest terms. And this largely due to the biblical teaching on the great tribulation. For instance, amillennial theologian Herman Hanko notes that postmillennialism "stands in sharp contrast with that whole body of biblical data which describes the days prior to the coming of Christ as days in which lawlessness abounds (Matthew 24:12)" and "Matthew 24 itself is strong proof of all this."[1] Premil

---

[1] Herman Hanko, "The Illusory Hope of Postmillennialism," *Standard Bearer* 66:7 (Jan. 1, 1990): 158. Herman Hanko, "An Exegetical Refutation of Postmillennialism" (Unpublished conference paper: South Holland, Ill.: South Holland Pro-

lennialist Wayne Grudem agrees: "Matthew 24 is such a difficult passage from the postmillennialist perspective."[2]

Any biblical eschatological system must be able to explain the great tribulation if it is to gain a hearing. But this is an especially important matter for postmillennialism due to its long-term, historical optimism. How can the postmillennialist propose an optimistic outlook for history if Christ, John, and other biblical writers warn of a time of great tribulation? The very idea of a great tribulation seems to conflict with the victorious outlook of postmillennialism.

In this chapter we will engage a brief overview of the Olivet Discourse. In the next chapter we will focus on the Book of Revelation. These overviews will serve two purposes: (1) They will interpret these large and important issues in biblical prophecy. (2) They will demonstrate how the great tribulation and the judgments of Revelation fit within the optimistic outlook of postmillennialism.[3]

The long-standing debate over Matthew 24 is unfortunate. When we look carefully at the prophecy it is not so difficult to comprehend it within a postmillennial scheme. One problem that modern evangelical laymen face is that Jesus' discourse is solidly rooted in the Old Testament. Unfortunately, they tend to be so New Testament oriented that they do not properly understand the Old Testament backdrop. We must remember that Jesus was speaking to a first-century Jewish audience steeped in the old covenant revelation (the Old Testament itself).

For our purposes in this book we will focus on the portion of the Olivet Discourse that relates to "the great tribulation." Undoubtedly, in our modern evangelical context of popular apocalypticism and interest in all things eschatological, this passage comes to people's mind as they ask: "Are we living in the last days?" "Is our day about to witness the fulfillment of these prophecies?"

---

testant Reformed Church, 1978), 27.

[2] Wayne Grudem, *Systematic Theology: An Introduction to Biblical Doctrine* (Grand Rapids: Zondervan, 1994), 1125.

[3] For fuller insights into this issue as appearing in Matt 24 see my books: *Perilous Times: A Study in Eschatological Evil* (Texarkana, Ark.: CMF, 1999), Thomas Ice and Kenneth L. Gentry, Jr., *The Great Tribulation: Past or Future?* (Grand Rapids: Kregel, 1999), and *The Olivet Discourse Made Easy* (Draper, Vir.: ApologeticsGroup, 2010).

This passage is familiar to most Christians. Who has not heard the dreadful prophecy of "wars and rumors of wars"? Or of "earthquakes in various places"? Or the alarming prospect of the "abomination of desolation"? Who has not feared the sound of "the great tribulation" reverberating from the lips of our Lord Jesus Christ? Unfortunately, though Matthew 24 is familiar to most, it is understood by few.

Most Christians in our generation and especially within modern evangelicalism, believe that we have just recently entered into the "last days." They often point to Matthew 24 as a signal to the beginning of the last days. They believe this text even offers signs indicating the great tribulation is about to explode on the scene, punctuating the end of the Church Age.

Bookstores and websites across America today are filled with end time scenarios that warn that the great tribulation in Matthew 24 and the events of the Book of Revelation are about to erupt all around us. They urge Christians to expect the imminent rapture of the Lord's people so that the great tribulation and Revelation's judgments might break forth. Books such as:

- Tim LaHaye and Craig Parshall, *Brink of Chaos* (2012) and *Edge of Apocalypse* (2010)
- Joel C. Rosenberg, *Damascus Countdown* (2013)
- Grant R. Jeffrey, *The New Temple and the Second Coming: The Prophecy That Points to Christ's Return in Your Generation* (2007) and *Countdown to the Apocalypse* (2008)
- Ron Rhodes, *The End Times in Chronological Order: A Complete Overview to Understanding Bible Prophecy* (2012)
- Ron Rhodes, *New Babylon Rising: The Emerging End Times World Order* (2019)
- John Hagee, *Four Blood Moons: Something Is about to Change* (2013).

These are only a few of the titles crowding the shelves of Christian bookstores and alarming Christians today. All of these books draw abundantly from the prophecies in Matthew 24 and, of course, related passages in the Book of Revelation.

How are we to understand this crucial discourse? What is "the great tribulation" of which Christ speaks in verse 21: "Then, there will be a great tribulation such as has not occurred since the beginning of the world, until now, nor ever shall be"?

In this study we will learn a remarkable fact: The great tribulation is *past*. Indeed, it occurred long ago in the first century and was concerned with the destruction of the temple in AD 70. Obviously, if this is so, then the great tribulation punctuated the *beginning* of Christianity (as the new covenant-phase of God's kingdom) and has no direct bearing on the *end* of the Church Age (supposedly lying in our near future). Thus, it does not contradict postmillennialism's historical optimism. Let us consider the evidence.

The Great Tribulation and Exegetical Demands

Most evangelicals focus on the remarkable judgments in the Matthew 24. And they do so to such an extent that they overlook important contextual clues that go against the popular conception of the great tribulation. And they do this despite the fact that these clues are quite clear and compelling.

These clues revolve around Matthew 24:34 which involves the key observation for a proper understanding of the great tribulation. This is the text we *must* focus upon; it will be our guiding star shedding light on our pathway through this dark and frightening passage. Let us note:

Literary setting

First, this verse links the great tribulation to the first century. Indeed, Christ specifically declares that the great tribulation will occur within the lifetime of his original audience. He clearly establishes the time frame in which it will come to pass: "Truly I say to you, this generation will not pass away until all these things take place" (Matt 24:34).

We find important interpretive evidence in the historical and contextual setting of Matthew 24 that helps us understand this statement. We must analyze Jesus' statement in its own historical and literary setting. That is, we must look back to Matthew 23 as the lead-in to Matthew 24. Let us see how this context helps our understanding.

In Matthew 23 Jesus calls down woes upon the scribes and Pharisees of *his generation* (Matt 23:13, 14, 15, 16, 23, 25, 27, 29). They are his antagonists; they are the backdrop against which his prophecy must be understood. As he concludes his woes section, he solemnly prophesies in Matthew 23:32: "Fill up, then, the measure of the guilt of your fathers." In other words, they are guilty; now they *will* fill up their final guilt.

An important reason motivates Jesus' denunciation of the Pharisees: they would be filling up the measure of the guilt of their fathers by attacking Christians. Notice Matthew 23:34–36:

"Behold, I am sending you prophets, and wise men, and scribes, some of them you will kill and crucify, some of them you will scourge in your synagogues, and persecute from city to city, that upon you may fall the guilt of all the righteous blood shed on the earth. Truly I say to you, *all these things will come upon this generation*."

The very setting in which Christ is delivering the Olivet Discourse is one of *impending* judgment *upon first-century Jerusalem*.

We must understand that the scribes and Pharisees live in a very important generation. Theirs was the time in which the Messiah comes. Tragically, "he came unto his own, and his own received him not" (John 1:11). First-century Israel lived in "the fullness of time" (Mark 1:15), but they missed its opportunity. They experienced the very era that "many prophets and righteous men desired to see" (Matt 13:17; cp. John 8:36), but were blind to it. They lived through "the time of your visitation," but "did not recognize" it (Luke 19:44). Indeed, Jesus "wanted to gather" them together in his care, but they "were unwilling" (Matt 23:37).

Thus, in Matthew 24:34, Jesus warns: "Truly I say to you, this generation will not pass away until all these things take place." The ones to whom he is speaking (his first-century disciples, Matt 24:1–2) will recognize the judgments in the Lord's great tribulation proclamation. This is a very clear and dogmatic statement.

We must note that he states here that *this generation* will *not* pass away until *all* these things take place. That includes the great tribulation mentioned in Matthew 24:21. Matthew 24:34 employs virtually identical language to the Matthew 23:36 statement regarding the soon-coming persecution of Christians: "Truly I say to you, all these things shall come upon this generation."

Historical setting

Second, this prophecy specifically focuses on the *first-century temple* toward which Jesus is physically facing. Let us notice what prompted the Olivet Discourse. In Matthew 23:37, 38, we read of a broken-hearted Savior lamenting:

"O Jerusalem, Jerusalem, who kills the prophets and stones those who are sent to her, how often I wanted to gather her children together, the way a hen gathers her chicks under her wings, and you were unwilling. Behold, *your house is being left to you desolate*."

The very Jerusalem sprawling before him (Matt 23:37a), the land where the prophets were killed while openly defying God (Matt 23:31), those people who had rejected his loving overtures (Matt 23:37b), that temple now being left desolate (Matt 23:38) — these are in Jesus' mind and upon his heart as he prophesies the great tribulation.

Notice his own disciples' response to his solemn declaration against the temple. Moments after his warning that their holy house was being left desolate, we read: "Jesus came out from the temple" (Matt 24:1). That was the very temple he had just declared is being left desolate (Matt 23:38). Then as he "was going away" from that first-century temple, his disciples "came up to point out the temple buildings to him" (Matt 24:1b). Then we read in Matthew 24:2:

> "Do you not see all these things? Truly I say unto you, not one stone here shall be left upon another that shall not be thrown down. And as he was sitting on the Mount of Olives, the disciples came to him privately saying, 'Tell us when shall these things be, and what will be the sign of your coming, and of the end of the age?'"

As a matter of historical and archaeological fact, that temple to which Jesus refers is destroyed in AD 70. No temple has existed in Jerusalem since that time. The Lord's prophecy relates to a temple that was actually destroyed just forty years later — a "generation" later (forty years = a generation; Num 32:13; Psa 95:10).

Specific command

Third, Jesus commands those particular people before him to do something. In Matthew 24:15 he discusses the "abomination of desolation" preparing his disciples for "the great tribulation" (Matt 24:21): "Let those who are in Judea flee to the mountains." Clearly this is not a worldwide phenomenon for he limits it to Jerusalem and Judea — because that is where the temple is located.

We know from history that the Jerusalem church heeded Christ's warning. They fled Jerusalem and went to Pella as the Jewish War with Rome broke out. The early church historian Eusebius (*ca.* AD 263–339) records this historical event:

> "The people of the church in Jerusalem had been commanded by a revelation, vouchsafed to approved men there before the war, to leave the city and to dwell in a certain town of Perea called Pella. And when those that believed in Christ had come thither

from Jerusalem, then, as if the royal city of the Jews and the whole land of Judea were entirely destitute of holy men, the judgment of God at length overtook those who had committed such outrages against Christ and his apostles, and totally destroyed that generation of impious men." (*Ecclesiastical History* 3:5:3)

In these three major lines of evidence we see that the focus of the great tribulation prophecy is on first-century Jerusalem and the temple. Regardless of contemporary "prophecy experts," the Lord locates the time of the great tribulation in a first-century event. Thus, in this one major argument we see that "the great tribulation" lies in our past.[4] But there is more.

The Great Tribulation and First-Century Facts

Since Jesus forthrightly declares that the great tribulation events will occur in the first century, we should expect to find evidence that they did in fact occur then. And we do! Let us survey a few of these. We will see the first-century historical fulfillment of several of his statements in Matthew 24.

False prophets

In Matthew 24:5 and 11 Jesus warns about false christs and prophets. That is, he is warning about the danger of false religious enthusiasts who will arise in an attempt to distract and disturb his disciples.

False religious leaders are an abundant problem in that day, as we see in the examples of Theudas (Acts 5:36), Simon (Acts 8:9, 10), and Paul's general warning to the Ephesian elders (Acts 20:29–30). For instance, Paul expresses his fear for the Ephesian church: "I know that after my departure savage wolves will come in among you, not sparing the flock; and from among your own selves men will arise, speaking perverse things, to draw away the disciples after them" (Acts 20:29–30).

The historical record of the first-century Jewish historian and priest Josephus (*ca.* AD 37–101) also documents false religious leaders who

---

[4] We should note that at Matt. 24:36 we have a topical transition indicator that shifts attention from AD 70 to the distant second advent, which AD 70 anticipates. The Greek phrase *peri de* ("now concerning") shows a change of subject (note especially Matt. 25:31–46). See: Gentry, *Olivet Discourse Made Easy*, ch. 8.

operated during the Jewish War with Rome which brought about the destruction of the temple: "such men deceived and deluded the people under pretense of divine inspiration" (*Jewish Wars* 2:13:4 §259). He speaks of others as "impostors and deceivers [who] persuaded the multitude to follow them into the wilderness and pretended that they would exhibit manifest wonders and signs" (*Antiquities* 20:8:6 §167–68).[5]

Clearly, Scripture and contemporary historical records testify of the very real danger of false religious teachers leading the Jews astray shortly after Christ dies.

Wars and rumors of wars

Matthew 24:6 and 7 speaks of "wars and rumors of wars." This is a sign that we constantly hear about today in eschatological discussions. Since there have always been wars, to which ones is Jesus referring? How is this rather broad sign helpful?

To understand the significance of this sign we must consider an important political fact of first-century history. When the Lord gave this sign to his audience they were experiencing the famous *pax Romana* (Latin for "the peace of Rome"). But what is this "peace of Rome"? And how is it significant for understanding Jesus' prophecy?

By military conquests and political savvy, the Emperor Augustus Caesar established this period of remarkable peace shortly before Christ was born (he was the reigning emperor when Jesus was born, Luke 2:1). This was an impressive time of widespread peace that enjoyed freedom from war. The first-century Jewish philosopher Philo (*ca.* 29 BC–AD 50) speaks of the Roman empire being "free from all sedition, and regulated by and obedient to admirable laws" (*Embassy to Gaius* 2:8). Roman naturalist and writer Pliny the Elder (who died in the eruption of Mount Vesuvius in AD 79) describes "the immeasurable majesty of the Roman peace" (*Natural History* 27:3). The third-century church father Origen (*ca.* 182– 254) mentions the "abundance of peace that began at the birth of Christ" (*Against Celsus* 2:30).

New Testament scholar, Bo Reicke, notes that "in the Roman Empire proper, the period of peace remains comparably undisturbed until the

---

[5] For an excellent academic study of this phenomenon, see: Rebecca Gray, *Prophetic Figures in Late Second Temple Jewish Palestine: The Evidence from Josephus* (Oxford: University Press, 1993), ch. 4

time of Nero."[6] The emperor Nero breached the *pax Romana* by engaging the Jewish War that resulted in the destruction of Jerusalem and the Jewish temple. Consequently, the Lord's prophecy offers a significant sign that warns Christians that despite the *pax Romana*, they will hear of "wars and rumors of wars" when "nation would rise up against nation."

When the Jewish War erupted in the late AD 60s, it broke the famous *pax Romana*. In this important war, Rome victoriously marched across Israel and mercilessly crushed that restive state. Though the Jewish Revolt initially flares up in late AD 66, the resulting formal war began in the Spring of AD 67. That was when Nero formally commissioned his general Vespasian to crush the revolt. As Josephus puts it: "Nero upon Cestius's defeat, was in fear of the entire event of the war, and thereupon made Vespasian general in this war" (*Jewish War* Pref., 8 §21; cp. 3:1:1–3 §1–8).

In that war Syria, Arabia, Egypt, and other nations aligned themselves against Israel. Josephus notes that Vespasian secured "a considerable number of auxiliaries from the kings in that neighborhood" (*Jewish War* 3:1:3 §8). He later writes:

"there were also a considerable number of auxiliaries got together, that came from the kings Antiochus, and Agrippa, and Sohemus, each of them contributing one thousand footmen that were archers, and a thousand horsemen. Malchus also, the king of Arabia, sent a thousand horsemen, besides five thousand footmen, the greatest part of which were archers; so that the whole army, including the auxiliaries sent by the kings, as well horsemen as footmen." (*Jewish War* 3:4:2 §68)

When Vespasian's son Titus took over the fight, Josephus mentions the greatly increased number of foreign national troops engaged in the siege of Jerusalem: "those auxiliaries that came from the kings, being now more in number than before, together with a considerable number that came to his assistance from Syria" (Josephus, *Jewish War* 5:1:6 §42).

But not only does this era experience the Jewish War, but it also resulted in a great and destructive civil war in Rome itself. In June of AD 68 Nero committed suicide as Rome erupts into civil upheaval and military strife (Josephus, *Jewish War* Pref., 9 §23). Britain, Germany, and Gaul revolt against Rome and seek to break out of the empire. Rome feared

---

[6] Bo Reicke, *The New Testament Era: The World of the Bible from 500 BC to AD 100* (Philadelphia: Fortress, 1964), 100.

that the Parthians from the East would mobilize because of the Empire's disarray during that time.

Roman historian Tacitus (AD 56–117) writes: "The history on which I am entering is that of a period rich in disasters, terrible with battles, torn by civil struggles, horrible even in peace. Four emperors failed by the sword; there were three civil wars, more foreign wars and often both at the same time" (*Histories* 1:2). He laments that "Rome and Italy are thoroughly wasted by intestine war" (*Hist.* 4:75). Josephus reports similarly that: "all was in disorder after the death of Nero" (*Jewish War* Pref. 1:2 §5).

Thus, both Jerusalem and Rome were experiencing nation arising against nation (Matt 24:7). These "wars and rumors of wars" (Matt 24:6) were truly signs for that first-century generation.

Famines in various places

Jesus continues with preparatory signs. In Matthew 24:7b he declares also that "in various places there will be famines." Famines are easy to document in biblical world of the first century where they were particularly devastating.

In Acts 11:28 we read of Agabus' prophecy of a "great famine" that occurs during the reign of Claudius (AD 50s): "There stood up one of them named Agabus and signified by the Spirit that there should be great famine throughout all the world: which came to pass in the days of Claudius Caesar." This is probably the famine Josephus mentions as striking Jerusalem: "A famine did oppress them at that time, and many people died for want of what was necessary to procure food withal" (*Antiquities* 20:2:5 §51).

Classical writers testify to the widespread, recurring famines in the AD 50s and into the 60s. We discover these in the works of Suetonius, Dio Cassius, Eusebius, and Orosius. For instance, speaking of Rome in AD 51 Tacitus writes: "This year witnessed many prodigies . . . . Further portents were seen in a shortage of corn, resulting in famine. . . . It was established that there was no more than fifteen days' supply of food in the city." (*Annals* 12:43)

As noted above Josephus speaks of the famine in Jerusalem (*Antiquities* 20:2:5) which he later calls "the great famine" (*Antiquities* 20:5:2 §101). He mentions others (*Antiquities* 20:5:2 §101; *Jewish War* 3:7:11 §180; 4:1:9 §62; 6:3:3).

Matthew 24:7c adds: "in various places there will be famines *and earthquakes.*" A particularly dreadful quake shakes Jerusalem in AD 67. Josephus records this frightful catastrophe: "There broke out a prodigious storm in the night, with the utmost violence, and very strong winds, with the largest showers of rain, and continual lightnings, terrible thunderings, and amazing concussions and bellowings of the earth, that was in an earthquake" (*Jewish War* 4:4:5 §286).

Tacitus mentions earthquakes in Crete, Rome, Apamea, Phrygia, Campania, Laodicea (of Revelation fame) and Pompeii during the time just before Jerusalem's destruction.[7] Severe earthquakes plague the reigns of the Emperors Caligula (AD 37–41) and Claudius (AD 41–54).[8] According to Seneca (ca. 4 BC—AD 65), others occur in Asia, Achaia, Syria, and Macedonia.[9] Of this era, Ellicott's commentary observes: "Perhaps no period in the world's history has ever been so marked by these convulsions as that which intervenes between the Crucifixion and the destruction of Jerusalem."[10]

Persecution and apostasy

In Matthew 24:9 and 10 Jesus warns of persecution and apostasy: "Then they will deliver you to tribulation, and will kill you, and you will be hated by all nations on account of My name. And at that time many will fall away and will deliver up one another and hate one another."

Almost every chapter of Acts details the persecutions the church endures in those early years: "And on that day a great persecution arose against the church in Jerusalem; and they were all scattered throughout the regions of Judea and Samaria, except the apostles" (Acts 8:1; cp. Acts 4:27; 16:20; 17:7; 18:12; 21:11; 24:1–9; 25:1–2).

Quite naturally a result of severe persecution is apostasy. John writes of apostasy in the first century: "They went out from us, but they were

---

[7] See Roman historians: Tacitus, *Annals* 2:47; 12:58 14:27; 15:22; Pliny, *Natural History* 2:86; and Suetonius, *Nero* 48; *Galba* 18. See also: Philostratus, *Life of Apollion* 4:11 and Orosius 7:7.

[8] W. J. Coneybeare and J. S. Howson, *The Life and Epistles of St. Paul*, 2 vols., (New York: Charles Scribner's, 1894), 1:126.

[9] Seneca, *Epistles* 91.

[10] Charles John Ellicott, ed., *Ellicott's Commentary on the Whole Bible* (Grand Rapids: Zondervan, n.d.), 6:146.

not of us; for if they had been of us, they would have continued with us; but they went out that they might be made manifest, that none of them were of us" (1 John 2:19; cp. 2 and 3 John). The Epistle to the Hebrews indicates a sizeable apostasy from among Jewish converts to Christianity (cf. Heb 2:1–4; 6:1–6; 10:26–31). Tacitus even alludes to apostasy during the Neronic persecution: "First, Nero had self-acknowledged Christians arrested. Then, *on their information*, large numbers of others were condemned" (Tacitus, *Annals* 15).

Conclusion

Thus, a quick survey of the biblical and the historical records show that many of the prophecies in Matthew 24 come to pass in the first century. This fits perfectly with the time-frame of Matthew 24:34 where our Lord asserts: "*this generation* shall not pass until *all* these things take place." Therefore, we see that postmillennialism is not negatively impacted by the great tribulation passage — thus far.

But problems arise in other texts within Matthew 24. So now we must consider the difficulties facing this first-century interpretation. These seem to be quite a bit more difficult to apply to the first century, and are often used to counter the preterist analysis made thus far.

The Great Tribulation and Interpretive Difficulties

Jesus expressly states that all these things shall occur in "this generation" (Matt 24:34). Regardless of how difficult a first-century fulfillment may seem for some of Jesus' statements, his clear time frame statement control our interpretation of the passage. Let us consider the troublesome issues that arise in the remaining prophecies.

Gospel proclamation

Many opponents of the first-century analysis point first of all to Jesus' statement regarding the preaching of the gospel: "And this gospel of the kingdom shall be preached in the whole world for a witness to all the nations, and then the end shall come" (Matt 24:14). How can we explain this statement? The "whole world" heard the gospel? This looks like a formidable objection against a first-century fulfillment. But looks are deceiving.

Actually, the meaning of the Greek word *oikumenē* ("world") here does not necessarily refer to the entire planet. We may glean many examples of a more restricted meaning from various Scriptures. For instance, in Acts 24:5 Luke records the Jewish opposition against Paul in that they charge him with causing dissension among the Jews "throughout the whole world." Surely this means *their* world, the world of their experience, the Roman empire.

But even more significantly the New Testament informs us that the gospel *is* preached throughout the entire known world of that day: "First, I thank my God through Jesus Christ for you all, because your faith is being proclaimed throughout the whole world" (Rom 1:8). Paul even writes that "the gospel ... has come to you, just as in all the world" (Col 1:6, cp. v 23). Interestingly, in this statement he uses the word *kosmos* which can and often does speak of the entire world. Yet he declares that the gospel has come "in all the world."

Thus, in the Matthew 24:14 Jesus simply states that the gospel will be preached in the entire *known* world of that day before these events reach their climax. That is, it will not be limited to Israel, as was his ministry (Matt 10:6; 15:24).

Abomination of desolation

What are we to make of his statement regarding the dreaded "abomination of desolation?" In Matthew 24:15 the Lord states: "Therefore when you see the abomination of desolation which was spoken of through Daniel the prophet, standing in the holy place." This prophecy is often associated with a world-ruling Antichrist in the future.

Contrary to popular opinion, though, this must also occur in the first century. We see this from the following evidence: (1) This "abomination" stands in the "holy place," i.e., the temple standing immediately before them (cp. Matt 23:38—24:2). (2) His audience could imagine no other locality, for Jerusalem is the "holy city" (Neh 11:1, 18; Isa 48:2; 52:1; Dan 9:24; Matt 4:5; 27:53) (3) Christ is responding to questions pertaining to that very temple (cf. Matt 24:1). He even points to the temple as he answers (Matt 24:2). That holy place will be dismantled by the Roman soldiers within forty years, a generation.

The "abomination of desolation" is the destruction of Jerusalem and the temple by pagan Roman armies. Luke's parallel account makes this clear. He takes Matthew's Hebraic language and interprets it for his Gentile audience: "But when you see Jerusalem surrounded by armies, then recognize that her desolation is at hand" (Luke 21:20). He tells us what the abomination is: Jerusalem being surrounded by Roman armies for the purpose of decimating her temple.

The Romans encircle Jerusalem on at least two occasions: under Vespasian in the initial siege and later under Titus not long before the Temple's final destruction. Of Vespasian's siege Josephus comments:

"And now the war having gone through all the mountainous country, and all the plain country also, those that were at Jerusalem were deprived of the liberty of going out of the city; for as to such as had a mind to desert, they were watched by the zealots; and as to such as were not yet on the side of the Romans, their army kept them in, by *encompassing the city round about on all sides*." (*Jewish War* 4:9:1 §490)

Josephus writes that later Titus builds "a wall round about the whole city" (*Jewish War* 5:12:1 §499).

After the first surrounding, the Christians are to flee from Judea. In God's providence, Vespasian withdraws from the siege when Nero dies; the Christians then had the opportunity to escape. The early church father Eusebius notes that:

"The people of the church in Jerusalem had been commanded by a revelation, vouchsafed to approved men there before the war, to leave the city and to dwell in a certain town of Perea called Pella. And when those that believed in Christ had come thither from Jerusalem, then, as if the royal city of the Jews and the whole land of Judea were entirely destitute of holy men, the judgment of God at length overtook those who had committed such outrages against Christ and his apostles, and totally destroyed that generation of impious men." (*Ecclesiastical History* 3:5:3; cp. Matt 24:16; Epiphanius, *Of Weights and Measures*, 15)

When the Roman soldiers finally obtain the upper hand in the temple, Josephus records how they raise their ensigns in the temple, bow to their to pagan deity, and offer incense to Caesar:

"The Romans upon the flight of the seditious into the city, and upon the burning of the holy house itself, and of all the buildings lying round about it, brought their ensigns to the Temple, and set them over against its eastern gate; and there did they offer sacrifices to them, and there did they make Titus imperator, with the greatest acclamations of joy." (*Jewish War* 6:6:1 §316)

The great tribulation

In Matthew 24:21 the Lord states that "then there will be a great tribulation, such as has not occurred since the beginning of the world until now, nor ever shall." Was AD 70 the worst catastrophe ever? What about World Wars I and II? Surely they were much worse than the first-century Jewish War with Rome. How can we explain this statement of Jesus while maintaining our first-century interpretation?

When we consider this in its biblical context, however, ample information supports my conclusion that A. D. 70 is in view. Note the following points.

First, Matthew 24:34 states that "all these things" shall occur in "this generation." We must notice that verse 34 appears just thirteen verses after verse 21. Therefore, "the great tribulation" must be one of "these things" to occur in "this generation."

Second, more catastrophic than our recent World Wars was Noah's Flood. And it must even be worse than the supposed future great tribulation. For in Noah's Flood the entire human population perished, except for one family (1 Pet 3:20; 2 Pet 2:5). And yet Jesus mentions Noah's Flood in his context (Matt 24:37–39). So something else must be going on here.

Third, to interpret Jesus properly we must understand the use of hyperbole in Old Testament prophetic language. Very often we find that judgment language in prophecy is formulaic, stock-in-trade, highly stylized, poetic language. For instance, in Exodus 11:6 we read these words regarding the tenth plague on Egypt: "'Moreover, there shall be a great cry in all the land of Egypt, such as there has not been before and such as shall never be again." Which is it? Is the great tribulation the worst judgment, as per Matthew 24:21? Or is the tenth plague upon Egypt the worst, as per Exodus 11:6?

In Ezekiel 5:9 we read of the Old Testament destruction of the temple by the Babylonians: "Because of all your abominations, I will do among you what I have not done, and the like of which I will never do again." But in Matthew 24 it happens again. This is apocalyptic, poetic, dramatic imagery.

In fact, Josephus evaluates the Jewish War similarly to Christ:
"Whereas the war which the Jews made with the Romans has been the greatest of all those, not only that have been in our time, but, in a manner, of those that ever were hear of, both of those wherein cities have fought against cities, or nations against nations" (*Jewish Wars*, Preface 1 §1).

"The misfortunes of all men, from the beginning of the world, if they be compared to these of the Jews, are not considerable as they were" (*Jewish Wars*, Preface, 4 §12).

"Neither did any other city ever suffer such miseries. . . from the beginning of the world" (*Jewish Wars* 5:10:5 §442).

Such comparative language is even used in more mundane, less dramatic circumstances in Scripture. Consider the sterling, high praise of both Hezekiah and Josiah — *from the same book*! Both are declared to be the best ever:

2 Kings 18:5 (Hezekiah)	2 Kings 23:25 (Josiah)
"He trusted in the LORD, the God of Israel; so that after him there was none like him among all the kings of Judah, nor among those who were before him."	"Before him there was no king like him who turned to the LORD with all his heart and with all his soul and with all his might, according to all the law of Moses; nor did any like him arise after him."

We even tend to use language in a similar, boldly exaggerated manner. This is like our saying to our child: "Haven't I told you a million times not to do this?" Or: "I have a ton of work to do." Or: "This will take me forever to straighten out."

Thus, Jesus' declaration in verse 21 is dramatic speech emphasizing the remarkable nature of this event. It is not meant to be literally understood.

Christ's coming

In Matthew 24:27 Jesus states: "For just as the lightning comes from the east, and flashes even to the west, so shall the coming of the Son of Man be." This is the sort of language we expect regarding the second coming of Christ, when he comes publicly and gloriously to conclude world history. Did Christ come like lightning in AD 70: How can this sort of language apply to AD 70?

We must understand this declaration in terms of the context. The Lord had just cautioned his disciples: "If therefore they say to you, 'Behold, He is in the wilderness,' do not go forth, or, 'Behold, He is in the inner rooms,' do not believe them" (Matt 24:26). We must recall Josephus' report in *Jewish Wars* 2:13:5 [261–62] cited above that records an episode in which an Egyptian false prophet arose in the wilderness claiming a great deliverance.

Jesus dismisses such by stating that when he physically comes again to the earth, it will be an unmistakable event: "For just as the lightning comes from the east, and flashes even to the west, so shall the coming of the Son of Man be" (Matt 24:27). The "for" (*gar*) here shows that he is giving the *reason* why his disciples should not think he is off in some wilderness or in an inner room somewhere. When he does return in his second coming, it will be as visible and dramatic as a lightning flashing.

So again, we see how the prophecies of Matthew 24 find fulfillment in the first century. In that these prophecies are for that era (Matt 24:34), why should we opt for a futurist approach to the matter?

The stars will fall

As the Lord continues in detailing the dramatic events, he states in Matthew 24:29: "But immediately after the tribulation of those days the sun will be darkened, and the moon will not give its light, and the stars will fall from the sky, and the powers of the heavens will be shaken." This sounds like the universe is collapsing. Did such literally occur in AD 70?

Once again we are facing apocalyptic, hyperbolic language. Consider Isaiah 13:10–13 which as instructive for this point:

"For the stars of heaven and their constellations will not flash forth their light; the sun will be dark when it rises, and the moon will not shed its light. Thus I will punish the world for its evil, and the wicked for their iniquity; I will also put an end to the arrogance of the proud, and abase the haughtiness of the ruthless. I will make mortal man scarcer than pure gold, and mankind than the gold of Ophir. Therefore I shall make the heavens tremble, and the earth will be shaken from its place at the fury of the Lord of hosts in the day of His burning anger."

Despite the initial appearance, Isaiah is *not* referring to the end of history. In the context he clearly identifies historical, Old Testament *Babylon* as the object of this judgment: "The oracle concerning Babylon which Isaiah the son of Amoz saw" (Isa 13:1). In verse 17 he also mentions the Medes as an element of God's judgment against them: "Behold, I am going to stir up the Medes against them." Not only are the Medes an Old Testament era people who no longer exist, but they would be meaningless if the preceding language speaks of some sort of cosmic catastrophe. Indeed, they themselves would fall under such catastrophic events.

This prophecy refers to Old Testament Babylon's overthrow, with the Median invasion securing that overthrow. The God of the universe is acting by his providential superintendence; metaphorically he is darkening the light of heaven on this might nation. The same imagery applies to the collapse of Jerusalem in AD 70 — which will occur "in this generation" (Matt 24:34) as the temple is destroyed (Matt 24:2).

Coming on the clouds

In Matthew 24:30 the Lord makes a remarkable statement. Unfortunately, the NASB, which we have been using throughout this book, is poorly translated here. So we will cite both the King James Version and the English Standard Version to better capture the meaning of the text.

In this verse we read a statement that sounds very much like the second coming of Christ. The KJV reads: "Then shall appear the sign of the Son of man in heaven: and then shall all the tribes of the earth mourn, and they shall see the Son of man coming in the clouds of heaven with power and great glory." The ESV reads: "Then will appear in heaven the sign of the Son of Man, and then all the tribes of the earth will mourn, and they will see the Son of Man coming on the clouds of heaven with power and great glory." Did Christ come on the clouds in AD 70?

This language certainly could be used of the second advent. But once again, just three verses later Jesus states very clearly and forcefully: "Truly, I say to you, this generation will not pass away until all these things take place" (Matt 24:34). Thus, we must recognize this as referring to the AD 70 event. A similarity of language between AD 70 and the second advent should not surprise us. After all, AD 70 is a distant reflection of that future, literal coming. Therefore the same dramatic language can apply to it, as well.

According to Jesus' prophecy there will be a "sign of the Son of Man in heaven." He is speaking of some sort of sign that he is at the right hand of God rather than in the cold hard ground. They will learn by some judgment sign that he is high and exalted, the one causing their judgment and anguish. This sign is (apparently) the smoke of the temple being destroyed. This will be the sign to the Jews that the Son of Man is no longer dead but in heaven at God's throne, where he will moves against them in judgment. He warned the Jews that this would happen (Matt 26:64). After all, he promised his disciples: "Truly I say to you, there are some of those who are standing here who will not taste death until they see the kingdom of God after it has come with power" (Mark 9:1).

Gathering the elect

Another confusing feature of Christ's prophecy is found in Matthew 24:31: "And He will send forth His angels with a great trumpet and they will gather together His elect from the four winds, from one end of the sky to the other." Is this speaking of the rapture? Did it occur in AD 70? Whatever this verse means, we must recall once again that Jesus affirms *only three verses later* that "all these things" will take place in "this generation" (Matt 24:34).

Actually it is important to understand that the word "angel" (Gk.: *aggelos*) can be (and often is) translated: "messenger." In Scripture it frequently refers to human messengers. We find this usage in Matthew 11:10; Mark 1:10; Luke 7:24 and 27. For instance, Jesus cites Malachi 3:1 as referring to John the Baptist: "This is the one about whom it is written, 'Behold, I send my *messenger* [*aggelos*] ahead of you, who will prepare your way before you'" (Matt 11:10).

Here Jesus is speaking of sending forth his messengers to trumpet the gospel of salvation. The collapse of the old covenant economy in the destruction of the temple is the sign that the gospel of God's saving grace is spreading to all the world. The messengers are overflowing the boundaries of Old Testament Israel (cp. Psa 147:19–20; Amos 3:2; Eph 2:11–12). God is finished with sacrifices and human priests (Heb 8:13); he will no longer confine his grace to a single nation (John 4:20–24). Now the gospel will go to all nations (Matt 28:18–20).

When the messengers go forth and declare the gospel, they go "from one end of the sky to the other," which means from one horizon (where the sky "touches" the ground) to the other, that is, in all directions (cp. Deut 4:32). They call people and gather them into a new body, the new covenant church of Christ. In fact, this "gathering" language appears in a very significant passage in Hebrews 10:25, where the Jews are commanded to "gather together" as Christians, and not to fall back into Judaism: "Not forsaking our own *assembling together*, as is the habit of some, but encouraging one another; and all the more, as you see the day drawing near."

Conclusion

As we have seen in this analysis of Jesus' teaching on the great tribulation, a strong case can be made that the tribulation is already past in that the destruction of Jerusalem and the temple in AD 70 is that great tribulation. The great tribulation ends the old covenant economy and establishes the new covenant order. As the writer of Hebrews expresses it: "When He said, 'A new covenant,' He has made the first obsolete. But whatever is becoming obsolete and growing old is ready to disappear" (Heb 8:13).

Therefore, the great tribulation lies in our past, not in our future. Postmillennialism does have a place for the great tribulation — at the *beginning* of Christian history, not at the end. The postmillennial outlook is not undermined by Christ's teaching on this time of terrible judgment.

REVIEW QUESTIONS FOR DISCUSSION

These questions deal directly with the material in this chapter. The answers can be found in the chapter.

1. The Bible speaks of "the great tribulation." How is that period believed to undermine the postmillennial hope?
2. When considering Jesus' teaching on the great tribulation it is important to consider exactly what he says. What is the key verse in Matthew 24 for properly understanding the great tribulation? How are we to understand that statement? Why was the first-century generation so important in redemptive history?
3. How do we know Jesus is speaking especially to his own generation of Jews regrading the great tribulation as a special tribulation for them? Provide evidence.
4. What sparks Jesus' great tribulation discourse? How is that so important for understanding the time and nature of the tribulation?
5. We see a particular, direct command to Jesus' original audience that makes the great tribulation directly relevant to them. What is that command? How does it help us in understanding the passage?
6. Discuss the significance of the sign regarding "wars and rumors of wars." How does a proper understanding of first-century history help us understand the direct relevance of this otherwise sign which appears too broad and general to be helpful as a sign.
7. Many opponents of the first-century interpretation of the great tribulation point to Jesus' statement that the gospel will "be preached the whole world" (Matt 24:14). This turns out actually to be helpful to the postmillennialist. Explain how this can be.
8. Probably Jesus' statement in Matthew 24:21 regrading the unparalleled nature of the tribulation is one of the leading objections to a first-century fulfillment of the great tribulation. How would you explain this statement to a non-postmillennialist expecting a future great tribulation?

The Truth about Postmillennialism

9. How does Christ come by lightning in a first-century great tribulation interpretation. What Scriptures would you use to prove this point?
10. How does the postmillennialist understand the angels gathering the elect from one end of heaven to the other?

STRETCHING FURTHER

1. Have you read any of the best-selling books on the great tribulation from a dispensational perspective? Did you once hold to that theology? Have you changed your opinion? What led you away?
2. Why is it so important to New Testament prophetic discussion that we understand the Old Testament first?
3. What is "apocalyptic literature"? What do we mean by "apocalypticism"?
4. What are some alternative interpretations of Matthew 24:34 that are brought forward to defend the interpretation of the great tribulation as lying yet in our future?
5. What were some new ideas you learned from this chapter?

Chapter 7
THE BOOK OF REVELATION IN POSTMILLENNIALISM

Undoubtedly, the most dramatic book in all of Scripture is John's Book of Revelation. Yet, despite being called "revelation" ("unveiling, uncovering"), Revelation is the most difficult book in the Bible. It is a work filled with great judgments and terrifying catastrophes. If it speaks of our future, then postmillennial optimism might well be unwarranted.

But does Revelation speak of our future? Since it mentions the "great tribulation" (Rev 7:14), perhaps it focuses on the same era of history as Jesus' Olivet Discourse: AD 70. As we will see, as a matter of fact, it does. This interpretation of Revelation is called "preterism," which is based on a Latin word that means "passed by," that is, it speaks of events that now lie in our already-completed past.

Obviously, we cannot deal with the whole of Revelation in this one chapter. Consequently, we will focus on just a few key matters necessary for understanding the book. We must first understand *when* John wrote Revelation, which will help us understand *what* Revelation is about. So let us open by noting:

The Early Dating of Revelation

In evangelical circles there are two basic schools of thought regarding when John wrote Revelation.

- The late-date view holds that John writes in AD 95–96, toward the end of the reign of the Emperor Domitian.
- The early-date view claims that John pens his great work just prior to the destruction of Jerusalem and the temple in AD 70, sometime between AD 65 and 70.

But which view is correct? And how is it significant for understanding John's message?

As we will see, a careful study of the evidence from within Revelation demands the early-date view. Although numerous lines of evidence push us in this direction, I will present just two particular evidences from the text of Revelation that strongly suggest the early-date view.[1]

The temple is still standing

The first line of evidence regards an architectural matter. When John writes Revelation the temple is still standing in Jerusalem, as we will see. If that is so, John must have written Revelation prior to AD 70. If John wrote it twenty-five years later, this would be a remarkable anachronism that would greatly confuse his original readers.

In Revelation 11:1–2 John receives a command from Christ (cp. Rev 11:3, 8) that assumes the temple is still standing:

"And there was given me a measuring rod like a staff; and someone said, 'Rise and measure the temple of God, and the altar, and those who worship in it. And leave out the court which is outside the temple, and do not measure it, for it has been given to the nations; and they will tread under foot the holy city for forty-two months.'"

This command presents us with a "temple of God" located in a "holy city." Scripture certainly calls Jerusalem a "holy city" (Neh 11:1–18; Isa 48:2; 52:1; Matt 4:5; 27:53). And Jerusalem is where God's temple was located (Mark 11:11, 15; Luke 4:9; Acts 22:17). How could John's audience surmise anything other than Jerusalem and its temple in this statement? And yet that temple was destroyed in AD 70. Thus, this prophecy must occur *before* that date. Hence, the early date of Revelation. But there is more.

Significantly, Revelation 11:2 parallels Jesus' statement in Luke 21:24:

Luke 21:24	Rev 11:2
"They will fall by the edge of the sword, and will be led captive into all the nations; and *Jerusalem* will be *trampled under foot* by the *Gentiles* until the times of the Gentiles be fulfilled."	"Leave out the court which is outside the temple, and do not measure it, for it has been given to the *nations* ["Gentiles" in Greek]; and they will *tread under foot* the *holy city* for forty-two months."

---

[1] For more detailed evidence, see my book *Before Jerusalem Fell: Dating the Book of Revelation* (3d. ed.: Chesnee, S.C.: Victorious Hope, 1998).

In Luke Jesus is certainly referring to the very temple existing in his day (Luke 21:5, 20), the temple which will soon fall (Luke 21:6, 31–32). From the strong similarities in language, John is obviously picking up on Jesus' prophecy, which requires that he too is referring to that same destruction. Thus, John must write Revelation before AD 70.

The sixth emperor is reigning
The second line of evidence involves an important political matter. When John writes Revelation Nero is reigning as the emperor in Rome. We may discern this from Revelation 17. In Revelation 17:1–6 John presents a vision of a seven-headed beast. In verses 9 and 10 an interpreting angel explains the meaning of the seven-headed beast:

"Here is the mind which has wisdom. The seven heads are seven mountains on which the woman sits, and they are seven kings; five have fallen, one is, the other has not yet come; and when he comes, he must remain a little while."

Here the angel informs John that the seven heads of the beast represent *both* seven mountains *and* seven kings. John would not naturally realize the double-meaning involved, so the angel helps him. Everyone agrees that the Book of Revelation is written sometime during Imperial Rome's oversight, whether prior to AD 70 or in the mid-90s or later. When the angel interprets the seven heads as representing "seven mountains," the reader would immediately understand this as referring to the famed seven hills of Rome. Thus, we have then a clear geographical reference to the ancient city of Rome.

Furthermore, the angel provides further interpretive insights by noting that the seven kings represent a succession of kings rather than seven kings reigning simultaneously: Five are in the past ("fallen"); one (obviously the sixth) is presently reigning ("one is"); and the other (the seventh) "has not yet come."

That five "have fallen" indicates they are no longer in power and are probably dead. That "one is" (present tense) indicates the sixth king is in power and actively ruling as John writes. The last one in the series of seven kings (obviously the seventh) "has not yet come" but "when he comes, he must remain a little while" after the sixth one passes from the scene. But who then are the seven successive kings whom John specifically enumerates?

Since the seven mountains (the seven hills of Rome) *also* reflect seven kings, we should expect that these seven kings involve Roman rule. Emperors ruled Rome in the first century and later. And the emperors are sometimes called "kings" (John 19:15; Acts 17:7). In fact, the emperor (or "Caesar") is mentioned in numerous texts (e.g., Mt 22:17; Mk 12:41; Lk 20:22; 23:2; John 19:12–15; Acts 17:7). Some emperors are specifically named in the New Testament, often for points of chronology: Augustus is the emperor when Jesus is born (Luke 2:1), Tiberius is the emperor when Jesus is crucified (Luke 3:1, and Claudius is the emperor during some of the key growth of the church in Acts (Acts 11:28; 18:2). Nero is clearly indicated in several references to "Caesar" (Acts 25:11ff; 26:32; 27:24; 28:19; Phil 4:22). Thus, in Revelation 17 the angel is informing John that these are emperors of the Roman Empire. But who is the "sixth"?

John is referring to the first seven emperors — emperors who are quite relevant to his original audience. Those emperors are:

Julius Caesar (49–44 BC)
Augustus (31 BC–AD 14)
Tiberius (AD 14–37)
Gaius (AD 37–41)
Claudius (AD 41–54)
Nero (AD 54–68)
Galba (June AD 68–January AD 69).[2]

Julius Caesar's military triumph begins the process of transforming Rome from a republic to an empire. Augustus firmly and formally establishes Rome as an empire and secures the *pax Romana*.

Now we must note that the angel tells John that the first five "have fallen" and that the sixth one "is." As a matter of historical fact, Nero is the sixth in the line of the Caesars. This demands that Nero is alive when John writes and that the composition of the book must have been prior to June 8, AD 68, the day Nero commits suicide as Rome erupts in civil war.

The angel then says, quite remarkably: "the other is not yet come and when he comes he will remain a short while." After Nero dies, the next Emperor is Galba, who rules from June to January, a period of only six

---

[2] This enumeration of the emperors (all called "Caesars" in honor of Julius Caesar) can be found in the Jewish historian Josephus (*Antiquities* 16:6:2; 18:2:2; 18:6:10), the Roman biographer Suetonius (*The Lives of the Twelve Caesars*), and the Roman historian Dio Cassius (*Roman History* 5).

months, the shortest reigning emperor to that time. Thus, after almost fourteen years of Nero's reign, we have the extremely short reign of Galba.

Since the events of Revelation "must soon take place" (Rev 1:1) because "the time is at hand" (Rev 1:3) this seventh emperor who has "not yet come" must appear *soon*, thus, within the context of John's audience. This insures that the series of seven kings must be the first seven emperors of the Roman empire.

Conclusion. These two lines of evidence — architectural (Jewish temple) and political (Roman emperors) — strongly indicate that John writes Revelation prior to the destruction of the temple (August/September, AD 70) and the death of Nero (June, AD 68). Because of this, the events of AD 70 could very well be those which John's prophecy anticipates.

But now let us consider:

The Historical Expectation of John

If we are to determine the meaning of Revelation, we need to search for any clues that might help us determine *when* John expects the events of Revelation to occur. As we look for the clues, it is vitally important that we understand the original audience and how they would read this book. Three factors will emphasize the historical circumstances of John's original recipients of this glorious composition.

Audience Relevance

One famous feature of Revelation is that he specifically addresses it to seven historical churches (Rev 1:4, 11; 2–3) and that he knows these churches quite well (Rev 2:2, 9, 13, 19, 23; 3:1, 3, 8, 15, 17). Scholars have discovered abundant evidence in the letters to the seven churches which show that he is familiar with detailed aspects of their culture, social standing, and historical circumstances in the first century world.[3]

Not only does he write to seven, well-known churches, but he writes in order to be understood: "Blessed is he who reads and *those who hear* the words of the prophecy, and *heed* the things which are written in it"

---

[3] See: Colin J. Hemer, *The Letters to the Seven Churches of Asia in Their Local Setting* (Grand Rapids: Eerdmans, 1989). W. M. Ramsey, *The Letters to the Seven Churches*, ed. by Mark W. Wilson (Peabody, Mass.: Hendrikson, rep. 1994 [1904]). Roland H. Worth, Jr., *Seven Cities of the Apocalypse and Greco-Asian Culture* (New York: Paulist, 1999).

(Rev. 1:3a). The idea of hearing the "words of the prophecy of this book" is not simply receiving audible intonations, but hearing with understanding — since must "keep" what he commands them.

Therefore, Revelation is directly relevant to the first-century churches who receive it. John does not write Revelation directly to the twenty-first century church almost 2,000 years later.

Furthermore, we should note that his original audience is already in "tribulation" (Rev 1:9). In Revelation 2 and 3 John highlights some growing problems the churches are facing (Rev 3:10). Some of their members are being tormented and killed (Rev 2:9–10, 13). Many are facing the onslaughts of Satan (Rev 2:13, 23). All must persevere through trying times (Rev 2:2–3, 19, 25; 3:10) that they must overcome (Rev 2:7, 11, 17, 26; 3:5, 12, 21).

Clearly then, John is writing to real Christians with their sandals firmly planted in the troublesome first-century scene. He is not taunting them about cobra helicopters or a future European Common Market. He is telling them about events that deal with their specific circumstances. Since they are in tribulation, they need to know what will become of them and the faith to which they have committed themselves.

Contemporary Expectation

The interpretation of Revelation must begin in the first chapter. John clearly expects the events of which he is writing to begin occurring *soon* — not two or more thousand years later. In fact, he repeatedly uses two strategically-placed terms to make this point.

In Revelation 1:1 John writes that these things "must soon take place." "Soon" is a translation of the Greek word *tachos*. It means what *all* the modern translations of Scripture affirm: the events are to "soon" to take place." The word also occurs at Rev 2:6; 3:11; 22:6, and in its adverbial form in Rev 22:6, 12, and 20.

John also adds "for the time is *near*" (Rev 1:3). The word for "near" is *engus*, which literally means at arm's length. This word occurs at Revelation 22:10 as well.

Clearly, the temporal impression that the original audience under tribulation and affliction would receive from this book is that John expects the events of his prophecy to occur "soon," because the time is "at hand." Not only does he utilize these two terms for this temporal expectation, but he also places them strategically in the book, at the beginning (Rev 1:1, 3) and conclusion (Rev 22:6, 10) of the book. Before one arrives at all the difficult imagery of the book, a very straightforward didactic portion indicates the immediacy of John's expectation.[4]

But note: What is it that he writing about for those first-century Christians to expect? This leads us to focus on:

The Literary Theme of Revelation

We do not have to look far to discover John's theme for his glorious work. In his very introduction John clearly states it: "Behold, He is coming with the clouds, and every eye will see Him, even those who pierced Him; and all the tribes of the earth will mourn over Him" (Rev. 1:7). But what does this mean?

As evangelical Christians we believe that Christ is coming again. And John's theme statement certainly sounds like he is referring to the Second Advent. We must understand that there is indeed a relationship between AD 70 and the final glorious coming of Christ. This is just as true in the similarities between the language here and that used for the Old Testament judgments on Babylon in Isaiah 13 and Idumea in Isaiah 34. All of these involve judgment actions of God in the realm of men, so we can expect similar language.

Yet this verse seems to point to God's judgment upon Jerusalem and her temple in AD 70.[5] As we consider this, the theme verse of Revelation, we must be alert to the fact that four verses prior to it, John states that these things are "near." And six verses before, he warns that these things are "soon to come to pass." This should alert us to the fact that he is not speaking of an event thousands of years distant. Nor is he referring to an event that could possibly occur soon. For he says that the events "*must soon take place*" (Rev 1:1), which should be expected "*for* the time is near" (Rev 1:3).

But besides the temporal expectation, how can we claim that this refers to AD 70, and not to the second coming of Christ? We will provide

---

[4] Though we do not have space to focus on the 1000 year reign of Christ in Rev 20, I would just note in passing that this is the one place in Revelation that looks beyond near-term events. The very nature of "a thousand years" (Rev. 20:1–6) requires this — if "soon" and "near" have any meaning. See the next note.

[5] For a more detailed presentation and defense of the view that Rev 1:7 refers to AD 70, see: Gentry, Kenneth L. Gentry, Jr., *The Book of Revelation Made Easy* (2d. ed.: Powder Springs, Geo.: American Vision, 2010), ch. 2.

three lines of evidence that indicate Revelation 1:7 teaches that Christ is coming in judgment upon the temple in the first century.

Coming with clouds

First, Revelation 1:7 mentions his "coming with the clouds." This is apocalyptic language which derives from Daniel 7:13, a heavenly vision of Christ in which he is given the keys of the kingdom *at his ascension* up to heaven. Daniel 7:13–14 reads:

"I kept looking in the night visions, / And behold, with the clouds of heaven / One like a Son of Man was coming, / And *He came up to the Ancient of Days* / And *was presented before Him*. / And to Him was given dominion, / Glory and a kingdom, / That all the peoples, nations, and men of every language / Might serve Him. / His dominion is an everlasting dominion / Which will not pass away; / And His kingdom is one / Which will not be destroyed."

The "cloud-coming" metaphor is common language among the poetically-inspired prophets of the Old Testament. It pictures a divine visitation of wrath upon historical nations who set themselves against God. When a nation falls, God is judging. Effectively God has "come" into the experience and realm of that nation, that is, Jehovah God has "come" to judge that nation. Isaiah 19:1 is a good parallel to Revelation 1:7:

"The oracle concerning Egypt. / Behold, the Lord is riding on a swift cloud, and is about to come to Egypt; / The idols of Egypt will tremble at His presence, / And the heart of the Egyptians will melt within them." (Isa 19:1)

Here In Isaiah 19 we learn that, according to Isaiah, God will "ride a swift cloud" — *into Egypt*. No commentator believes that God actually rides a cloud down into Egypt, becomes visible, and lays it waste by some sort of perceivable action. They all agree that it is a symbolic, apocalyptic reference to God judging Egypt in the Old Testament.

Consequently, if apocalyptic language will allow us to understand a divine judgment in history as a cloud-coming, then this possibility is open to us in Revelation 1:7. And John does declare that these events are "near" at hand. Metaphorically-speaking Christ will come upon a cloud in judgment soon.

Moreover, the parallel in Matthew 21:33–45 makes the Jerusalem reference certain. Even dispensational scholars interpret this prophetic parable as referring to AD 70. Christ asks: "when the owner of the vineyard *comes*, what will he do to those vine-growers?" (Matt 21:40). The answer he elicits from his audience is: "he will bring those wretches to a wretched end" (Matt 21:41). Then in Matthew 21:43 he declares that the kingdom of God will be taken away from the Jewish nation: "Therefore I say to you, the kingdom of God will be taken away from you, and be given to a nation producing the fruit of it" (Matt 21:43).

The leaders of Israel clearly understood his point, for we read: "when the chief priests and the Pharisees heard His parables, they understood that He was speaking about them" (Matt 21:45). Jesus is hear teaching that the chief priests would lose their beloved temple and place of authority. Thus Matthew 21 uses "coming" language for the destruction of Jerusalem. John is utilizing the same "coming" language in Revelation 1:7.

Those who pierced him
Second, Christ is coming against "those who pierced him." Here we must ask: who are those who pierced him? According to the New Testament record it is especially the first-century Jews. They are the ones who deliver him for crucifixion and cry out for his death (Matt 20:18–19 Mark 15:13; Luke 23:21; John 19:6). They refuse to allow Pilate to let him go, even though Pilate protests vehemently against their treachery (Matt 27:24; John 19:6, 15). They call the curse of his blood upon themselves (Matt 27:25). In short, the Jews of the first century demand Christ's crucifixion; and his blood does come down upon them and their children in that generation.

Throughout the New Testament record, the primary covenantal onus of Christ's death falls upon the Jews, even though the Romans were the physical agents involved. In Acts 5:30 Peter blames his Jewish kinsmen for crucifying Christ: "The God of our fathers raised up Jesus, whom *you* had put to death by hanging Him on a cross" (cf. Acts 2:36). This kind of language is repeated time and again in Acts 3:13–15; 7:52; 10:39; 13:27–29; Acts 26:10; and 1 Thess 2:14–15.

So then, according to Scripture the ultimate responsibility for Jesus' death falls upon the Jewish nation in the first century. They demand it; they cause it; they are blamed for it. This fits perfectly with the exposition of Revelation 1:7 we are presenting.

The tribes of the earth
Third, "all the tribes of the earth will mourn." The Greek word for "earth" (Gk., *gē*) can either mean "earth" or "land." In fact, "the land" is

a famous designation for Israel's land, the promised land of the Jews (Gen 12:1; 13:15–17; 15:7; Deut 34:4; Josh 21:43; Psa 105:11; Acts 7:3). The idea of "the land" is something precious to the Jew.

In addition, when you think of Israel, you think of its division into the twelve tribes (Gen 49:28; Exo 24:4; Eze 47:13; Matt 19:28; Luke 22:30; Acts 26:7). In fact, John mentions those twelve tribes in Revelation 7:4–8 and 21:12 (cp. Rev 5:5).

So, what John says here is: "Jesus whom you crucified is coming to judge you, and all the tribes will mourn as a result of the judgment. His judgment will be a public event of a great and grievous proportions."

Thus, Revelation's theme is Christ's judgment on all the tribes of the land for causing Christ's death. This surely refers to AD 70 when they forever lose their temple.

The Evil Characters in Revelation

Revelation is not presented in mundane narrative discourse. Rather, John writes it as a drama with vivid, terrifying imagery. Before we can trace the movement of Revelation, we should consider two major characters we encounter there: the beast and harlot.

The seven-headed beast

Audience relevance requires that these people be living during the time of Rome, and that the image must refer to something in their own historical time frame. As with the seven heads of the beast referring to both seven mountains and seven kings (Rev 17:9–10), so here we must understand this beast imagery in a two-fold manner. The *generically* refers to its corporate reality and *specifically* to an individual representative of the corporate entity.

Generically, the beast represents Rome, the empire as such. The beast has seven heads which are seven mountains, which clearly describes the city of Rome. The beast's arising from the sea portrays Rome sending its legions from across the Mediterranean Sea into Israel. The ten diadems (crowns) on the beast's head represent political power, with which Rome was well-endowed.

As all commentators recognize — even dispensationalists such as Walvoord, Ryrie, and Thomas[6] — the image of the beast shifts between this corporate, national power and a specific representative of that power. One of the heads, or kings, "is" (Rev 17:10). The one that "is" is the sixth emperor of Rome, Nero. Interestingly, Nero fits the facts in many remarkable ways.

In Revelation 13:18 the number of the beast is "the number of a man": 666 (in the Greek: "six hundred and sixty and six," *not* a series of three sixes, "six and six and six"). Hebrew, John's native language (which scholars recognize colors the grammar of Revelation), does not have a separate numbering system. They use the letters of the alphabet as numbers, with the first ten letters representing the values of 1–10, then follow the values of 10, then 100s. When you add up the first-century letters that make up the Hebrew name "Neron Kaiser," you find that it adds up to 666. Scholars have documentation of this spelling in Hebrew from the New Testament era.

Furthermore, Nero was the first imperial persecutor of the Christian Church, which Revelation 13:7 anticipates: "it was also given to him to make war with the saints and to overcome them." According to historical records, his persecution breaks out in November of AD 64 and does not cease in finality until his death in June of AD 68. This happens to be a period of roughly forty-two months, as per Revelation 13:5: "There was given to him a mouth speaking arrogant words and blasphemies, and authority to act for forty-two months was given to him."

In addition, in Revelation 13:10 we read of the sword death of the beast: "If anyone is destined for captivity, to captivity he goes; if anyone kills with the sword, with the sword he must be killed." Nero commits suicide by ramming a sword in his own throat. According to the Roman biographer Suetonius (AD 70–130), he "drove a dagger into his throat, aided by Epaphroditus, his private secretary" (*Nero* 49; cp. Tacitus, *Ann.* 16:14).

In Revelation 13:3 we have further proof for the Rome-Nero identity of the beast. Revelation's beast has a head that dies, causing the beast to crumple to its death. But, surprisingly, the beast arises again to amaze

---

[6] Robert L. Thomas, *Revelation 8-22: An Exegetical Commentary* (Chicago: Moody, 1995), 158; John F. Walvoord, *The Revelation of Jesus Christ* (Chicago: Moody, 1966), 199–200; Charles Caldwell Ryrie, *Revelation* (Chicago: Moody, 1968), 82.

the world. Interestingly, after Nero dies Rome experiences a rapid succession of four emperors, the famous "Year of the Four Emperors" (Galba, Otho, Vitellius, and Vespasian). During this period the empire is in catastrophic turmoil. Its tributary nations attempt to escape Roman authority. It looks to all as if Rome is dying. Contemporary Roman historian Tacitus writes: "This was the condition of the Roman state when Galba entered upon the year that was to be for Galba his last and for the state almost the end" (*Histories* 1:11).

But what happens? The Roman beast revives! Suetonius informs us in his *Lives of the Twelve Caesars*: "The empire which for a long time had been unsettled and drifting through the usurpation and violent death of three emperors, was at last taken in hand and given stability by the Flavian family" (*Vespasian* 1). Vespasian assumes the emperorship, revives it, and the empire arises from its death throes to live once again.

Thus, the whole world, as it were, is surprised at the remarkable change of circumstances. Josephus reports: "So upon this confirmation of Vespasian's entire government, which was now settled, and upon the *unexpected* deliverance of the Romans from ruin" (*Jewish War* 4:11:5 §657). Rome's civil war was so ruinous that everyone is surprised by her recovery.

Thus, the evidence demands that the beast is first-century entity: the Roman Empire ruled over by the evil Nero Caesar. This fits well with the temporal indicators (Rev 1:1, 3) and the thematic statement in Revelation 1:7.

The great harlot

Many would tell us that the harlot who sits on the beast is the city of Rome, because Rome is, after all, seated on seven hills (cf. Rev 17:3, 9). The beast, however, is already Rome — so this identification would be redundant. Actually, this woman is probably Jerusalem. She "sits" on the seven hills of Rome *in that* she relies on imperial Rome to get at Christianity (Luke 21:12; Acts 17:1, 6–7). We must recall how the Jews rely upon the Roman judicial apparatus to crucify Jesus (Matt 20:18–19; John 19:6, 12, 15). This is the "sitting" John mentions in Revelation 17. Several lines of evidence suggest that the harlot is Jerusalem.

First, in several places in Revelation Babylon is called the "great city" (Rev 14:8; 16:19; 17:18; 18:2, 10, 16, 18, 21). But what is this "great city"? We find the first mention of "the great city" in Revelation 11:8. There John defines it "mystically" as "Sodom and Egypt," but geographically as "the place where also their Lord [Jesus] was crucified," which was Jerusalem (see Matt 20:17–19; Luke 24:18–20). Elsewhere we see writers referring to Jerusalem as "great." Jeremiah writes: "And many nations will pass by this city; and they will say to one another, 'Why has the Lord done thus to this great city?'" (Jer 22:8). Josephus laments Jerusalem's fall: "Where is now that great city, the metropolis of the Jewish nation?" (*Jewish War* 7:8:7 §375).

Second, the Babylonian harlot is "full of the blood of the saints" (Rev 16:6; 17:6; 18:24). Certainly, Rome had recently begun persecuting the saints. The evidence suggests, however, that Jerusalem is a better identification of the harlot at this point, for the following reasons:

(1) Throughout Acts, Jerusalem is the persecutor of Christianity (e.g., Acts 4:3; 5:18; 8:1; 9:1–2). (2) The theme of Revelation is the judgment upon "the tribes of the Land," i.e., Israel (Rev 1:7) — those tribes are specifically named in Revelation 7:4–8. Babylon's judgment appears in great detail in Revelation 17 and 18. If Revelation's theme pertains to Jerusalem, so do the judgments that fulfill the theme. Hence, the judgments on "Babylon" are really judgments on Israel. (3) The slain Lamb appears twenty-seven times in Revelation (e.g., Rev 5:6, 12; 13:8). He is seeking vengeance upon his slayers. In Matthew 27:35, the Jews assume the guilt of the Lamb's blood, calling down a covenantal curse upon themselves.

Third, in Revelation 17:4 John describes the Babylonian harlot's dress as containing gold and purple and scarlet colors. These reflect the Old Testament high priest's robe (Exo 28:5–6) and the tabernacle/temple decoration (cf. Exo 26:1; 36:8). John is picking up on high priest / temple imagery to portray the harlot. Jerusalem's worship has been prostituted by rejecting their Messiah. In fact, Jesus calls first-century Israel "an adulterous generation" (Matt 12;39; 16:4).

Fourth, the harlot has an evil inscription on her forehead: "upon her forehead a name was written, a mystery, 'Babylon the Great, the Mother of Harlots and of the Abominations of the Earth'" (Rev 17:5). John appears to present this as a negative image of the high priest who had something positive written on his forehead: "Holy to the Lord" (Exo 28:36–38). John presents the high priest because he represents the temple, which stands at the heart of Jerusalem and Israel. Readers in that day would have made associations with the temple. Interestingly, Jeremiah also accuses Old Testament Israel of having "a harlot's forehead" (Jer 3:3).

Fifth, in Revelation 17 and 21 John compares two women: the harlot (historical Jerusalem) and the bride of the Lamb, which is called the "new" and "heavenly Jerusalem" (Rev 21:2). Paul likewise makes this comparison between the earthly, literal Jerusalem and the heavenly Jerusalem of Christianity (Gal 4:24–26). The writer to the Hebrews utilizes the same comparison (Heb 12:18–22). Under the guise of two women, John is setting Israel (Judaism) against Christianity (the Church, the bride of Christ, 2 Cor 11:2; Eph 5:25–32). The following evidence clearly demonstrates his intentional comparison:

(1) The same angel comes to John to reveal both the harlot and the bride (Rev 17:1 with 21:9). That angel presents both to John in the same way. (2) The two women have a contrasting character, one is negative, one positive (Rev 17:1 with 21:10). That is one is a negative reflection of the other. (3) The two women are set in contrasting environments (Rev 17:3 with 21:10), which bespeak their relationship but difference.

Sixth, in Revelation John calls Jerusalem by pagan names. In Revelation 11:8 she is called "Sodom and Egypt." In Revelation 2:9 and 3:9 Jesus (speaking in the letters to the churches) declares the Jews have no right to the name "Jew" because their synagogues are "synagogues of Satan." Thus, we should not be surprised in John's applying the name "Babylon" to Jerusalem. Sodom, Egypt, and Babylon were enemies of God in the Old Testament. John's rhetorical point is that since Jerusalem crucified the Messiah and persecuted his followers, she is acting as immorally as the enemies of God in the Old Testament. We should note also that John is following Jesus' lead in his rhetorical denunciations, for Jesus also denounces Israel's cities by negatively comparing them to Old Testament pagan cities, such as Tyre, Sidon, and Sodom (Matt 10:15; 11:20–24//).

Seventh, Revelation is the most Old Testament-flavored book in the entire New Testament. It cannot be understood apart from this background. In the old covenant economy, Israel was God's bride or wife (Isa 54:5a; cp. Isa 50:1; 62:4; Jer 2:2; 3:14, 20; 31:32; Hos 1:2; 2:2,7, 16; 5:4; 9:1, 10). God graciously married this nation, i.e., entered into covenant with her. For instance, in Jeremiah 31:32, where the new covenant is revealed, God complained: "They broke my covenant though I was a husband to them."

Israel, however, is an unfaithful wife who commits harlotry by chasing after foreign gods (Eze 23; Mal 2:11). Accordingly, God sends his lawyers, the prophets, to warn her. They bring a "case," a legal brief, against her (cf. Hos 4:1; Mic 6:2). On the basis of God's law, God calls forth witnesses against his faithless wife (Isa 1:2, 21; cp. Deut 4:26; 30:19). The same problem existed in the Old Testament as we encounter in the New — marital infidelity on Israel's part.

All of this covenant imagery and the legal actions involved in them bear upon the application of the judgments in Revelation against Israel. In Revelation 4, prior to the announcement of the judgment, John sees God seated on his throne. Forty-seven of the sixty-two times "throne" appears in the New Testament are found in Revelation. Within Revelation we find much language of judicial judgments: "judgment," "witnesses," "wrath," and so forth.

Why is God seated upon the throne and why does so much judicial imagery appear in Revelation? Because God is legally divorcing his harlotrous wife Israel. He intends to take a new bride, the church. The scroll, therefore, in Revelation 5 is a bill of divorce against Israel who has become an adulteress (cf. Matt 12:39; 16:4). John is picking up on imagery that Jeremiah has already utilized (Jer 3: 1, 8; cp. Isa 50:1). Jeremiah was writing about the original Babylonian captivity that resulted in the destruction of Israel's first temple. John is writing of a new Babylon that causes the second temple to be destroyed: Jerusalem, the apostate wife of God (cf. Matt 23:27–24:2). The seven-sealed scroll indicates a sevenfold judgment upon his adulterous wife, as per Old Testament warnings (cf. Lev 26:18, 21, 24, 28). God will now capitally punish her for her capital crime (Rev 14:8, 17–20; 16:6–7; 18:1–19:4).

At the end of Revelation we see a vision of the new bride. Thus, after he legally disposes of his adulterous wife, God turns to take a new wife. In Revelation 21:10 John sees the new city coming down out of heaven. This bride is a "new Jerusalem," who fills the void left by the demise of the old Jerusalem. Therefore, Revelation is teaching us of God's divorce of Israel because she had committed a final, horrible transgression for which he must divorce and punish her.

Israel will experience a glorious renewal in the plan of God when God at last raises her dry bones from covenantal death in conversion (Eze 37; Rom 11:12–15). But Revelation warns and explains of her first-century judgment, an historical event about to occur in the lifetimes of the original recipients of the book (Rev 1:1, 3; 22:6, 10).

Conclusion

Revelation's dramatic, catastrophic imagery might seem to undermine the postmillennial hope. Yet upon closer inspection, it does nothing of the kind. The Book of Revelation has near-term time indicators (Matt 24:34; Rev 1:1, 3; 22:6, 10) tying its events to the first century. This period of chaos and catastrophe did lie in the future when John wrote. But they lay in his *near* future. They are the "birth pangs" (Matt 24:8) of the kingdom, not its death throes.

REVIEW QUESTIONS FOR DISCUSSION

These questions deal directly with the material in this chapter. The answers can be found in the chapter.

1. What are the two leading options for the date of John's writing Revelation? How is the dating of Revelation significant to its interpretation?
2. Remember how significant the temple and sacrificial system was for old covenant Israel and even for Jesus and the earliest Christians. How is the reference to the temple in Revelation 11 significant for the book's interpretation?
3. The seven heads of the beast is an important element in discovering the date of Revelation's composition. Explain how this is helpful.
4. Jesus' Olivet Discourse and John's Revelation are closely related. Both speak of the "great tribulation," both have the same theme (Matt 24:30; Rev 1:7), both mention the temple, and both provide statements that tie them to the first century. Where are the leading temporal statements in Revelation that link the book to the first century? How is their variation and placement significant to the discussion?
5. Revelation's theme appears to be the coming judgment upon Israel for rejecting their Messiah (Rev 1:7). This theme sounds like it could be speaking of the second coming of Christ. Present the argument that it really refers to the AD 70 destruction of the temple.
6. What does Revelation's seven-headed beast represent? Provide evidence for this interpretation.
7. What does Revelation's great harlot represent? Provide evidence for this interpretation.
8. Discuss the covenant imagery of Israel's relationship to God in the Old Testament and how that helps us understand the significance of the great harlot.

The Truth about Postmillennialism

9. How can we believe that John would call Jerusalem Sodom, Egypt, Babylon, and a harlot? Where might we discover evidence that this sort of name calling does occur in Scripture?
10. Revelation is the most Old Testament-flavored book in the New Testament. How does this help with properly interpreting the book as a judgment upon Israel?

STRETCHING FURTHER

1. Can you think of other biblical books whose interpretation depends on understanding its dating?
2. Had you known about this view of Revelation before? When did you first hear of this approach, and how long did it take it to sink in so that you changed your view or Revelation?
3. Since Revelation 20:6 appears immediately after the description of the new Jerusalem coming down out of heaven (Rev 21:1–22:5), how might the postmillennial preterist interpret this? Clues: see Galatians 4:25–26; Heb 12:22–29. See the divorce imagery in God's Old Testament relationship to Israel that is mentioned in this chapter.
4. Have you read any good books presenting and defending this view of Revelation? Which ones would you recommend?
5. What were some new ideas you learned from this chapter?

Chapter 8
INTERPRETIVE LITERALISM IN POSTMILLENNIALISM

A quick check of any Christian bookstore, or the turning of the dial to any Christian radio station shows that dispensational premillennialism is by far the most popular prophetic outlook in the Church today. Because of this, competing eschatologies such as postmillennialism have a difficult time getting into popular discussion. This is one of the reasons for presenting postmillennialism as the first in the *Truth About Series* of books.

Because of the prevalence of dispensational thinking, one of the leading issues in prophetic discussion is: How shall we interpret Scripture? Dispensationalists capture the hearts and minds of evangelicals by claiming to employ plain and simple literalism in interpreting prophecy. Unfortunately, this literalistic principle does not work. In this portion of our study we will see why.

Leading dispensationalist theologian Charles C. Ryrie sets forth interpretive literalism as an absolutely essential component of biblical interpretation which (in his view) leads unfailingly to dispensationalism. He writes: "Dispensationalists claim that their principle of hermeneutics is that of literal interpretation. . . . The dispensationalist claims to use the normal principle of interpretation *consistently* in *all* his study of the Bible."[1]

Ryrie gives three arguments for the literalistic hermeneutic.[2]
1. "Philosophically, the purpose of language itself seems to require literal interpretation. . . . If God be the originator of language and if the chief purpose of originating it was to convey His message to man, then it must follow that He, being all-wise and all-loving, originated sufficient language to convey all that was in His heart to tell man. Furthermore, it

---

[1] Charles C. Ryrie, *Dispensationalism* (2d. ed.: Chicago: Moody, 1995), 80, 82.
[2] Ryrie, *Dispensationalism*, 81–85.

must also follow that He would use language and expect man to use it in its literal, normal, and plain sense."[3]
2. "Prophecies in the Old Testament concerning the first coming of Christ — His birth, His rearing, His ministry, His death, His resurrection — were all fulfilled literally. There is no non-literal fulfillment of these prophecies in the New Testament."[4]
3. "If one does not use the plain, normal, or literal method of interpretation, all objectivity is lost."

Despite the dispensationalists' vigorous assertions, "consistent literalism" is an impossible ideal. In fact, recent dispensationalists are beginning to admit this and are developing a new form called "progressive dispensationalism."[5] For instance, John S. Feinberg, a noted contemporary dispensationalist, complains regarding hermeneutics: "Ryrie is too simplistic."[6] Craig Blaising and Darrell Bock agree, lamenting Ryrie's "conceptual naivete."[7]

---

[3] Benware expresses it: "Literal interpretation assumes that, since God wants His revelation understood by people, He based His revelatory communication on the normal rules of human communication." Paul N. Benware, *Understanding End Times Prophecy: A Comprehensive Guide* (Chicago: Moody, 1995), 19.

[4] See also: Thomas Ice in *PSB*, 1312. John F. Walvoord in Roy B. Zuck, ed., *Vital Prophetic Issues: Examining Promises and Problems in Eschatology* (Grand Rapids: Kregel, 1995), 19–20. Charles L. Feinberg, *Millennialism: The Two Major Views* (3rd ed. Chicago: Moody, 1980), 41. J. Dwight Pentecost, *Things to Come: A Study in Biblical Eschatology* (Grand Rapids: Zondervan, 1958), 10. Robert P. Lightner, *The Last Days Handbook* (Nashville: Thomas Nelson, 1990), 126–127.

[5] The earliest form of dispensationalism from John Nelson Darby (1800–82) to Lewis Sperry Chafer (1871–1952) is known as "Classic Dispensationalism." Charles Ryrie (b. 1925) brought the first major shift in this eschatological perspective, creating what is called "Revised Dispensationalism." The most recent view is that of Craig Blaising (b. 1949) and Darrell L. Bock (b. 1953) is "Progressive Dispensationalism." Ryrie's Revised Dispensationalism is the dominant view, promoted by Hal Lindsey, Tim LaHaye, and many other popular writers.

[6] John S. Feinberg, ed., *Continuity and Discontinuity: Perspectives on the Relationship Between the Old and New Testaments* (Westchester, Ill.: Crossway, 1988), 73.

[7] Craig A. Blaising and Darrell L. Bock, eds., *Dispensationalism, Israel and the Church: The Search for Definition* (Grand Rapids: Zondervan, 1992), 29.

One major theologian who left dispensationalism is former Dallas Theological Seminary professor S. Lewis Johnson. He warns of the anti-apostolic nature of literalism, which he says interprets "woodenly."[8]

Let us consider a few problems for the Ryrie-style "consistent" literalist.

The Philosophy of Language Argument

The most disconcerting point about Ryrie's first proof is that it is preconceived. This is quite evident in Ryrie's statement that "principles of interpretation are basic and ought to be established before attempting to interpret the Word."[9] In other words, you must adopt your method of interpretation before you even open Scripture.

Clearly Ryrie's approach disallows even the possibility of a figurative or spiritual interpretation *at the very outset* of the interpretive inquiry. Why must we begin with the literalist assumption? May we not suspect that *several* interpretive approaches are necessary for so large and rich a work as the Bible? After all, is it not dedicated to a lofty and spiritual theme (the infinite God's redemption of sinful man) and written by so many authors (at least thirty-nine) in so many portions (sixty-six books) over such a long period of time (1,500 years)? Should we not suppose that such a work might employ a variety of literary genres?

Indeed, as noted Old Testament scholar J. A. Alexander observed long ago regarding the claim that prophecy (for instance) must always be interpreted literally: "to assert, without express authority, that prophecy must always and exclusively be one or the other, is as foolish as it would be to assert the same thing of the whole conversation of an individual throughout his lifetime, or of human speech in general."[10]

To make matters worse, even popular dispensationalist writers themselves admit that the Bible often employs figures of speech. But this brings up the very controversy before us: *when* is prophecy to be interpreted literally, and when figuratively?

Vern Poythress rightly suspects that dispensationalists "may have conveniently arranged their decision about what is figurative *after* their

---

[8] S. Lewis Johnson, *The Old Testament in the New* (Grand Rapids: Zondervan, 1980), 83.

[9] Ryrie, *Dispensationalism*, 79.

[10] J. A. Alexander, *Commentary on the Prophecies of Isaiah* (Grand Rapids: Zondervan, rep. 1977 [1875]),1:30.

basic system is in place telling them what can and what cannot be fitted into the system. The decisions as to what is figurative and what is not figurative may be a product of the system as a whole rather than the inductive basis of it."[11]

Interestingly, Ryrie inadvertently proves Poythress' observation. Ryrie writes: "The understanding of God's differing economies is *essential* to a proper interpretation of His revelation within those various economies."[12] In other words, you must already have a dispensational framework ("understanding God's differing economies") in order to do "proper interpretation."[13]

In addition, Ryrie's first argument actually ends up begging the question. He claims that because God created language, "the purpose of language itself seems to require literal interpretation" on the basis that "it must . . . follow that He would use language and expect man to use it in its literal, normal, and plain sense."[14] He continues explaining this by declaring that "language was given by God for the purpose of communication with humankind. Therefore, God would give His linguistic communication in the most understandable way — literally and normally."[15]

---

[11] Vern S. Poythress, *Understanding Dispensationalists* (Grand Rapids: Zondervan, 1987), 53. For a discussion between Poythress and two leading dispensationalists over Poythress' arguments, see: *Grace Theological Journal* 10:2 (Fall 1989): 123–160.

[12] Ryrie, *Dispensationalism*, 29.

[13] This is despite Ryrie's complaint: "Thus the nondispensationalist is not a consistent literalist by his own admission, but has to introduce another hermeneutical principle (the 'theological' method) in order to have a hermeneutical basis for the system he holds." Ryrie, *Dispensationalism*, 84.

[14] A problem of which dispensationalists seem to be unaware is the question as to *whom* a prophecy is "plain." The dispensational practice is to try to make it plain to the 20th-century reader. What about the ancient audience to whom it was written?

[15] Ryrie, "Dispensationalism," in Mal Couch. ed., *Dictionary of Premillennial Theology* (Grand Rapids: Kregel, 1996), 94. Pentecost follows suit: "Inasmuch as God gave the Word of God as a revelation to men, it would be expected that His revelation would be given in such exact and specific terms that His thoughts would be accurately conveyed and understood when interpreted according to the laws of grammar and speech. Such presumptive evidence favors the literal interpretation, for an allegorical method of interpretation would cloud the meaning of the message delivered by God to men." Pentecost, *Things to Come*, 10.

This is not very convincing, given that God often communicates in Scripture through poetry, metaphor, parable, and other literary means — as even dispensationalists admit.

The First-coming Fulfillment Argument

Ryrie states that "the Old Testament prophecies concerning Christ's birth and rearing, ministry, death, and resurrection were all fulfilled literally."[16] This part of the argument for literalism is one of the most frequently employed and one of the most compelling arguments available. The argument, though, is more influential among laymen than scholars. Biblical scholars recognize that it suffers from the informal logical fallacy of question-begging. That is, it assumes what it supposed to prove.

In fact, former Dallas Theological Seminary professor J. Dwight Pentecost holds that this is "one of the strongest evidences for the literal method." He vigorously asserts: "When the Old Testament is used in the New it is used only in a literal sense." Indeed, he claims that "no prophecy which has been completely fulfilled has been fulfilled any way but literally."[17]

Unfortunately, the New Testament does not support this bold claim. This clearly involves question-begging, for to say that all prophecies transpiring in the New Testament are fulfilled literally requires that one's system *already be in place*. Literalism *definitionally* writes off all non-literal fulfillments in advance.

This first-coming argument ignores Old Testament kingdom prophecies fulfilled in the *ministry of Christ*. These are not fulfilled literally as a political conception. For instance, Jesus declares: "But if I cast out demons by the Spirit of God, then the kingdom of God has come upon you" (Matt 12:28; cp. Luke 17:20–21).These kingdom prophecies are clearly fulfilled in the first century, for we learn that: "after John had been taken into custody, Jesus came into Galilee, preaching the gospel of God, and saying, 'The time is fulfilled, and the kingdom of God is at hand; repent and believe in the gospel'" (Mark 1:14–15).

We must recognize that the kingdom prophecies expect the Spirit's outpouring to accompany the coming of the kingdom (Isa 32:14–17; Eze

---

[16] Ryrie, "Dispensationalism," in *Dictionary of Premillennial Theology*, 94.
[17] Pentecost, *Things to Come*, 10–11. See also: H. Wayne House and Thomas D. Ice, *Dominion Theology: Blessing or Curse?* (Portland, Ore.: Multnomah, 1988), 321–323.

36:25–27; Joel 2:28ff). And this effusion of the Spirit, most definitely comes to pass in the first century as a consequence of Christ's redemptive work (Acts 2:1–20; cf. cf. John 7:39; 16:12ff).

Even apart from the debate regarding Christ's kingdom, the dispensationalist argument is unfounded. For instance, although Matthew often interprets Old Testament prophecies literally, *he does not always do so.* Crenshaw and Gunn carefully demonstrate that "out of 97 OT prophecies only 34 were directly or literally fulfilled, which is only 35.05 percent."[18] They show that the New Testament presents many examples of non-literal fulfillment.

Examples of non-literal fulfillment in the Gospels are easy to come by. For example, Matthew employs typological fulfillment when he states that God's calling Israel up out of Egypt (Hos 11:1) was fulfilled when the young Jesus returned from his flight to Egypt (Matt 2:15). This is certainly not a literal exposition of Hosea 11:1. The prophet Hosea is clearly speaking of Israel as God's son, for "Israel is My son, My firstborn" (Exo 4: 22–23).

Matthew also presents us with analogical fulfillment (fulfillment by something similar occurring). We see this when Bethlehem weeps for her children killed by Herod (Matt 2:18), which fulfills Rachel's weeping for her children (Jer 31:15). Matthew declares that in this event, the word "spoken through Jeremiah the prophet was fulfilled" (Matt 2:17). This is most certainly *not* a literal fulfillment.

These examples alone destroy Ryrie's bold claim "the Old Testament prophecies concerning Christ's birth and rearing, ministry, death, and resurrection were all fulfilled literally."

The Objective Interpretation Argument

Because of the alleged "objectivity" factor, dispensationalists commonly deem any non-literal interpretation of Scripture as evidence of encroaching liberalism. We may note Ryrie's comments in this regard:

> "Although it could not be said that all amillennialists deny the verbal, plenary inspiration of the Scriptures, yet, as it will be shown later, it seems to be the first step in that direction. The

---

[18] Curtis I. Crenshaw and Grover Gunn, *Dispensationalism Today, Yesterday, and Tomorrow* (Memphis, Tenn.: Footstool, 1985), 22. See their helpful chart on pages 14–22. For an excellent analysis of the matter, see: David E. Holwerda, *Jesus and Israel: One Covenant or Two?* (Grand Rapids: Eerdmans, 1995).

system of spiritualizing Scripture is a tacit denial of the doctrine of the verbal, plenary inspiration of the Scriptures. . . . Thus the allegorical method of amillennialism is a step toward modernism."[19]

Ryrie would also apply his concern to postmillennialism. This argument is not at all persuasive.

Interpretive literalism does not protect orthodoxy

We may easily point out that many *cults* approach Scripture literalistically — and erroneously.

Consider the premillennial cult of Mormonism. They teach that God has a literal, tangible body. After citing Genesis 1:26–27 regarding Adam's creation "in the image and likeness of God," LeGrand Richards, a former Apostle of the Church of Jesus Christ, Latter-day Saints, writes: "Attempts have been made to explain that this creation was only in the spiritual image and likeness of God. . . . Joseph Smith found that he was as literally in the image and likeness of God and Jesus Christ, as Seth was in the likeness and image of his father Adam."[20]

Consistent literalism is held inconsistently

In Malachi 4:5–6 we read the following prophecy: "Behold, I am going to send you Elijah the prophet before the coming of the great and terrible day of the Lord." And he will restore the hearts of the fathers to their children, and the hearts of the children to their fathers, lest I come and smite the land with a curse." Yet some leading dispensationalists state that it is not necessary to hold to a literal return of Elijah before the end.

Pentecost writes regarding Malachi's statement: "The prophecy is interpreted by the Lord as being fulfilled, *not in literal Elijah*, but in one who comes in Elijah's spirit and power."[21] Walvoord recognizes the problem but hesitates: "It was clear that Elijah was a type of John and to some extent that John the Baptist fulfilled Elijah's role. But, predictively,

---

[19] Charles C. Ryrie, *The Basis of the Premillennial Faith* (Neptune, N.J.: Loizeaux, 1953), 34, 35, 46.

[20] LeGrand Richards, *A Marvelous Work and Wonder* (Salt Lake City: Dessert, 1950), 16.

[21] Pentecost, *Things to Come*, 311–313; cf. E. Schuyler English, "The Two Witnesses," *Our Hope* 47 (April 1941): 666.

it is difficult to determine whether the future one will come in the spirit and power of Elijah or be Elijah himself."[22]

On their "consistent" literal hermeneutic, why should this be "difficult"? Does not Walvoord himself open this very book with these words: "Unmistakably, the evidence is overwhelming that God means exactly what He says as prophecy after prophecy has already been literally fulfilled"[23]? Thus, this leading, scholarly advocate of the literalistic approach to Scripture breaches his own declared principle of literalism — and in a book that *opens* with his expressly stated declaration that we must interpret Scripture literally.

Regarding the supposed millennial era, Ezekiel 43:19 states: "'You shall give to the Levitical priests who are from the offspring of Zadok, who draw near to Me to minister to Me,' declares the Lord GOD, 'a young bull for a sin offering." But *The New Scofield Reference Bible* suggests regarding this prophecy of a renewed "sin offering" that "the reference to sacrifices is not to be taken literally." How can this be?

But when literalism supports their eschatological system, dispensationalists vigorously argue for it. For instance, of Isaiah 9:7 the *New Scofield Reference Bible* explains: "'The throne of David' is an expression as definite, historically, as 'the throne of the Caesars,' and does not admit of spiritualizing."[24] Yet dispensationalist Gordon H. Johnston writes: "God will fulfill His promises in the Davidic covenant (2 Sam. 7:8–16) to establish the eternal Davidic dynasty over Israel through a single ideal Davidic King who will reign eternally (Ps. 89:20–37)."[25] But when we read this passage we discover it expressly mentions *David* himself, not a "Davidic King": "I have found David My servant; / With My holy oil I have anointed him, / With whom My hand will be established; / My arm also will strengthen him" (Ps 89:20–21).

---

[22] John F. Walvoord, *Prophecy Knowledge Handbook* (Wheaton, Ill.: Victor, 1990), 339–40.

[23] Walvoord, *Prophecy Knowledge Handbook*, 7.

[24] *New Scofield Reference Bible*, 721. Poythress cites many examples of non-literalism in the notes of the original *SRB*: Gen 1:16; 24:1; 37:2; 41:45; 43:45; Exo 2:2; 15:25; 25:1, 30; 26:15; Eze 2:1; Zech 10:1; John 12:24. Poythress, *Understanding Dispensationalists*, 24 n.

[25] Gordon H. Johnston, "Millennium: Old Testament Descriptions of," in *Dictionary of Premillennial Theology*, 269.

Pentecost states that "the promises in the Davidic covenant concerning the king, the throne, and the royal house are fulfilled by Messiah in the millennial age." To support this he lists Ezekiel 34:23–25 and Hosea 3:5 as evidence.[26] H. A. Ironside writes regarding the Ezekiel passage: "I do not understand this to mean that David himself will be raised and caused to dwell on the earth as king. . . . The implication is that He who was David's Son, the Lord Christ Himself is to be the King."[27] More recently the *Tim LaHaye Prophecy Study Bible* commented on Ezekiel 34:22–26: "this will be David's great descendant, Jesus."

This is remarkable in light of what Ezekiel and Hosea actually state. Ezekiel declares: "And I, the Lord, will be their God, and *My servant David* will be prince among them; I, the Lord, have spoken" (Eze 34:24). Hosea reads: "Afterward the sons of Israel will return and seek the Lord their God and *David their king*." How can these specific references to "David" (*not* "David's son," or "one of David's descendants") actually mean "Christ" — in a strictly literalistic system? On what basis can a consistent literalist allow this view? Where is the literalism in this?

The Emmaus disciples of our Lord held to the then-prevailing, literalistic Jewish conceptions of the Messianic kingdom. Regarding Jesus' death they lament: "But we were hoping that it was He who was going to redeem Israel. Indeed, besides all this, it is the third day since these things happened" (Luke 24:21). Because of this Jesus must open the Scriptures to them to show them their error (Luke 24:25–27, 32, 45).

Christ rejects the Jews' literalistic *political Messianism* (Matt 23:37–38; Luke 19:41–42; 24:21–27; John 6:15; 18:36). The early disappointment and confusion among Jesus' earliest followers and the general Jewish rejection of Jesus as Messiah are at least partially due to the problem that "the prevailing method of interpretation among the Jews at the time of Christ was certainly the literal method of interpretation."[28]

We see this problem operating when Christ confronts Nicodemus about his confusion regarding Jesus' statement he needs to be "born again" (John 3:3–4). In his answer, Jesus points to this very interpretive practice: "Jesus answered and said to him, 'Are you the teacher of Israel,

---

[26] Pentecost, *Things to Come*, 476.

[27] Harry A. Ironside, *Expository Notes on Ezekiel the Prophet* (New York: Loizeaux, 1949), 262. Cf. Charles C. Ryrie, *The Basis of the Premillennial Faith* (Neptune, N.J.: Loizeaux, 1953), 88. Walvoord, *Prophecy Knowledge Handbook*, 60.

[28] Pentecost, *Things to Come*, 17.

and do not know these things? . . . If I have told you earthly things and you do not believe, how will you believe if I tell you heavenly things?'" (John 3:10, 12).

Jesus continually rebuts literalism during his ministry

John's Gospel is clear evidence of this, presenting virtually a case study in the error of literalism. In John 2:19–21 Jesus is speaking of his body-temple being destroyed and rising again, but the Jews think he is talking about the literal "temple." As already noted, in John 3:5–7 Nicodemus thinks Jesus' reference to being "born again" requires that a man literally re-enter his mother's womb.

In John 4:10–15 Jesus is speaking to the woman at the well about spiritual water, whereas the woman thinks he is referring to literal water. In John 4:31–38 Jesus says he has food to eat, which makes his disciples think he is referring to physical food, not spiritual sustenance. In John 6:31–35, 51–58 Jesus calls himself "bread" that men must eat and refers to drinking his blood, which his audience thinks are calls to cannibalism.

In John 8:32–36 Jesus talks about being spiritually "free," but his audience think he is speaking of breaking from physical slavery. In John 8:51–53 promises that those who keep his word will never die, which his hearers interpret to mean they will never *physically* die. In John 9:39–40 Jesus speaks of being "blind," which makes the Pharisees think he is speaking about physical blindness. In John 11:11–14 Jesus states that Lazarus is "sleeping," but "Jesus had spoken of his death, but they thought He was speaking of literal sleep." In John 13:33–37 Jesus informs his disciples that he will soon be leaving (by which he means "dying"), but Peter thinks he is physically traveling somewhere else.

On and on we could go: literalism led the Jews astray, leading to their rejecting Christ. While he hung on the cross "the people stood by, looking on. And even the rulers were sneering at Him, saying, 'He saved others; let Him save Himself if this is the Christ of God, His Chosen One'" (Luke 23:35).

Conclusion

Interpreting Scripture requires more than simply pursuing "literalism." We have seen samples from Scripture itself which prove that we cannot approach every Scripture with a literalistic assumption. To claim "consistent literalism" is not only to be extremely naive, but is to promote a falsehood. Even dispensationalists are not consistently literal.

REVIEW QUESTIONS FOR DISCUSSION

These questions deal directly with the material in this chapter. The answers can be found in the chapter.

1. In modern lay circles what is the most popular interpretive approach to Scripture? Summarily state the dispensational argument for literalism based on the philosophy of language.
2. Summarily state the dispensational argument for literalism based on the first-coming fulfillments.
3. Summarily state the dispensational argument for literalism based on the objectivity argument.
4. How can we respond to Ryrie's argument that we should expect Scriptural to be literal because of the philosophy of language as a means for communication?
5. Explain how Ryrie's argument about the philosophy of language appears to beg the question, that is, to be circular?
6. Explain how Ryrie's argument that all the first-coming prophecies are fulfilled literally is ultimately circular and therefore invalid.
7. Regarding Ryrie's claim that the first-coming prophecies are fulfilled literally, how can we show that literalism does not protect orthodoxy?
8. Regarding Ryrie's claim that the first-coming prophecies are fulfilled literally, how can we show that literalism is held inconsistently?
9. Regarding Ryrie's claim that the first-coming prophecies are fulfilled literally, how can we show that Jesus rejected literalist interpretations? Give two samples proving your answer.
10. Why do you suspect that the overall literalism argument is persuasive to so many Christians?

STRETCHING FURTHER

1. Who are some leading proponents of the literal interpretation?
2. Did you ever hold to the literalist principle of interpretation? What passage or argument led you away from that position?
3. Can you offer samples from your reading of dispensational literature that illustrate their inconsistency in applying the literalist principle?
4. Have you ever tried to present postmillennialism to someone who adamantly rejected your view due to its not being literal? Explain the situation.

5. What were some new ideas you learned from this chapter?

Chapter 9
ISRAEL IN POSTMILLENNIALISM

Because of the prominence of dispensationalism and the Left Behind phenomenon in evangelical circles, it is important for us to reflect on a fundamental emphasis in contemporary prophecy discussions: Israel. This is also important in that Israel plays a prominent role in Scripture.

As all Christians know, throughout most of the Old Testament Israel is God's special people — beginning in seed form with the calling of Abraham in Genesis 12. She is God's elect nation (Deut 7:7–8 ; 10:15; Zech 2:8; Rom 3:1–3; 11:1) and the focal point of his redemptive mercies in history (Deut 4:7–8; Psa 147:19–20; Amos 3:2; Rom 9:4). Because of her commanding presence in old covenant history and her central role in Old Testament prophecy she becomes a crucial issue in understanding the Bible.

Dispensationalism's Error Presented

Perhaps *the* leading distinctive of dispensational theology is that ethnic Israel *remains* God's key and favored people who will continue to star in his major plan for history. This view of Israel involves dispensationalism in its most destructive error. All of dispensational theology orbits around Israel as its theological center of gravity.

Two of the most destructive results of dispensationalism's error regarding Israel are: (1) Their view of Israel destroys the unity of God's people by creating two peoples of God in history (Israel and the church). (2) Their prophetic expectation built on Israel lowers the status of the church (by exalting geo-political Israel) and retrogressively re-institutes blood sacrifices as history's final and highest redemptive period (the millennium).

Let us focus briefly on this error as explicated by dispensationalism's leading scholar, Charles C. Ryrie. Ryrie points to the centrality and exaltation of Israel as the *first* of the three essential elements of dispensationalism: "*A dispensationalist keeps Israel and the Church distinct.*"[1] He defends this position over against all other evangelical theologies by arguing that:

---

[1] Charles C. Ryrie, *Dispensationalism* (2d. ed.: Chicago: Moody, 1995), 39.

"(1) The Church is not fulfilling in any sense the promises to Israel. (2) The use of the word *Church* in the New Testament never includes unsaved Israelites. (3) The Church Age is not seen in God's program for Israel. It is an intercalation. (4) The Church is a mystery in the sense that it was completely unrevealed in the Old Testament and now revealed in the New Testament. (5) The Church did not begin until the day of Pentecost and will be removed from this world at the rapture which precedes the Second Coming of Christ."[2]

Unfortunately, each one of Ryrie's points is mistaken. As a result, the dispensational house is built on sinking sand. Let us see how this is so.

Dispensationalism's Error Demonstrated

Scripture does not support Ryrie's distinctive assertions, which are absolutely fundamental to the dispensational system. Rather, it teaches that old covenant Israel is the *seed* of God's people which flowers in history, becoming the expanded, global people of God in the new covenant Church.

Some call this view "replacement theology" and fear that this position altogether removes Israel from God's plan and *replaces* her with a new and distinct people. But a better description would be to call it "fulfillment theology." That is, this view understands the new covenant as *expanding* God's people from a single ethnic people embodied in a geo-political structure to a pan-ethnic people embodied in a new structure, the new, true, spiritual, covenant Church.

The more common evangelical and Reformed of the oneness of God's people recognizes old covenant Israel as the *actual* people of God in the Old Testament. Their they function as the *seed* of the coming global people of God in the New Testament. As the Westminster Confession of Faith (written in the 1640s) expresses it, Israel is "a church under age" (WCF 19:3).

Let me demonstrate the biblical warrant for this "fulfillment theology" view.

1. The Old Testament anticipates the expansion of God's people. The Old Testament writers foresee a time in which God will expand his people by bringing blessings on the Gentiles and including them within Israel. This

---

[2] Charles C. Ryrie, *The Basis of the Premillennial Faith*, (Neptune, N.J.: Loizeaux, 1953), 136.

hope is established early in Israel's formative history when God establishes his covenant with Abraham: "As for Me, behold, My covenant is with you, / And you shall be the father of a *multitude of nations*" (Gen 17:4).

Perhaps the clearest and more remarkable expression of this appears in Isaiah 19:23–25. There we read that God will include Israel's greatest enemies in his covenant:

"In that day there will be a highway from Egypt to Assyria, and the Assyrians will come into Egypt and the Egyptians into Assyria, and the Egyptians will worship with the Assyrians. In that day Israel will be the third party with Egypt and Assyria, a blessing in the midst of the earth, whom the Lord of hosts has blessed, saying, 'Blessed is Egypt My people, and Assyria the work of My hands, and Israel My inheritance.'"

Zechariah expresses this hope by referring to Israel's earliest enemy within the Promised Land:

"And a mongrel race will dwell in Ashdod, / And I will cut off the pride of the Philistines. / And I will remove their blood from their mouth, / And their detestable things from between their teeth. / Then they also will be a remnant for our God, / And be like a clan in Judah, / And Ekron like a Jebusite." (Zech 9:6–7)

The conversion of the Gentiles in the new covenant is simply the fulfillment of these prophecies which adopt Israel's enemies into her family.

2. The New Testament applies Old Testament prophecies to the church. In Jeremiah 31:31 we read of God's prophecy of the new covenant with Israel: "'Behold, days are coming,' declares the LORD, 'when I will make a new covenant with the house of Israel and with the house of Judah." Christ inaugurates this "new covenant" toward the end of his ministry as he establishes the New Testament phase of his church. During his Last Supper he states: "This cup which is poured out for you is the new covenant in My blood" (Luke 22:20).

Dispensationalist J. Dwight Pentecost is quite correct when he writes of Christ's establishing the Lord's Supper: "In its historical setting, the disciples who heard the Lord refer to the new covenant . . . would certainly have understood Him to be referring to the new covenant of

Jeremiah 31."[3] What could be more obvious? The prophecy of God's new covenant with Israel applies to the New Testament church.

In fact, the sudden appearance of the "new covenant" in the New Testament record without qualification or explanation, demands that it refer to Jeremiah's well-known new covenant (see: Matt 26:28; Mark 14:24; Luke 22:20; 1 Cor 11:25). Paul even promotes the new covenant as an important aspect of his ministry: God "also made us adequate as servants of a new covenant" (2 Cor 3:6). Thus, he is a minister of the new covenant *even though he is the "apostle to the Gentiles"* (Rom 11:13; cp. Acts 9:15; 22:21; 26:17; Rom 1:5; 15:16; Gal 1:16; 2:7; Eph 3:1, 8; 1 Tim 2:7; 2 Tim 4:7).

In Acts 15 James speaks of the conversion of the Gentiles as a fulfillment of a distinctively Jewish-sounding prophecy in Amos 9:11–12. James sees in the conversion of the Gentiles a rebuilding of "the tabernacle of David":

> "Simeon has related how God first concerned Himself about taking from among the Gentiles a people for His name. 'And with this the words of the Prophets agree, just as it is written, "After these things I will return, / And I will rebuild the tabernacle of David which has fallen, / And I will rebuild its ruins, / And I will restore it, / In order that the rest of mankind may seek the Lord, / And all the Gentiles who are called by My name," / Says the Lord, who makes these things known from of old.'" (Acts 15: 14–18)

Thus, he sees the converted Gentiles as enter the prophetic "tabernacle of David," thereby sharing in this Jewish promise.

During her rebellion in the Old Testament, God promises "the sons of Israel" that "in the place / Where it is said to them, / 'You are not My people, ' / It will be said to them, / 'You are the sons of the living God'" (Hos 2:10b). Paul cites this glorious prophecy of inclusion in God's family and directly applies it to the church:

> "even us, whom He also called, not from among Jews only, but also from among Gentiles. As He says also in Hosea, 'I will call those who were not My people, "My people," / And her who was not beloved, "beloved."' / And it shall be that in the place where

---

[3] J. Dwight Pentecost, *Things to Come: A Study in Biblical Eschatology* (Grand Rapids: Zondervan, 1958), 126.

it was said to them, "you are not My people," / There they shall be called sons of the living God.'" (Rom. 9:25–27)

3. The new covenant church receives Old Testament promises. Not only do we learn that Old Testament prophecies regarding Israel are fulfilled in the church, but we even see that old covenant *promises* for Israel apply to the church. The new covenant church is the recipient of old covenant Israel's blessings.

For instance, when Paul speaks to the *Gentiles* in Ephesians, he reminds them that "formerly" they were "at that time" in the past "strangers to the covenants of promise" (Eph 2:12). That is, in their *past* they were devoid of God's "promise." But this no longer is true!

Paul adds: "but now in Christ Jesus you who were *formerly* were far off have been brought near" (Eph 2:13). Interestingly, Paul is citing Isaiah 57:19, which was a promise of future blessing to Israel given though she was currently in sin. In Isaiah 56:1 through 66:24 Isaiah is focusing on the shame and glory of *Zion*, that is to be followed by her glory. Yet Paul applies a promise from Zion in Isaiah 57:19 to the Gentiles in Ephesus.

In Galatians 3:29 he refers to the foundational promise to Israel contained in the Abrahamic Covenant. He applies that promise to the Gentiles: "if you belong to Christ, then you are Abraham's offspring, heirs according to promise."

Dispensationalists teach that the new covenant church is an aside, an intercalation in God's major plan, a parenthesis in the outworking of redemptive history. The New Testament, however, deems her the direct recipient of God's full blessings.

4. The new covenant church is not a mystery wholly unrevealed. Based on Ephesians 3, dispensationalist argue that the new covenant era, international church was a mystery that is "completely unrevealed in the Old Testament." Certainly the clarity of the revelation of God's expanding people increases in the New Testament. But that revelation *was*, in fact, given in the Old Testament.

Let's look at dispensationalism's key passage for this concept. Ephesians 3:5–6 reads: "which in other generations was not made known to the sons of men, as it has now been revealed to His holy apostles and prophets in the Spirit; to be specific, that the Gentiles are fellow heirs and fellow members of the body, and fellow partakers of the promise in Christ Jesus through the gospel." We have already seen that the Old Testament anticipated this. Now we must note that Ryrie and the dispensationalists misread Paul's statement. Consider the following.

To begin with, we must discern *for whom* the revelation was a mystery. Ephesians 3:3–6 reads: "By revelation he made known unto me the mystery . . . which in other ages was not made known unto *the sons of men*." Thus, the "mystery" now revealed was not previously made known to the "sons of men," that is, the Gentiles. It *was* made known to the "sons of Israel" through their prophets. The phrase "sons of Israel" appears often in the Old Testament (e.g., Exo 3:3, 14–15; 4:31; 5:14–15; 6:5; etc.), setting them over against the rest of the world, the Gentiles, the "sons of men." When God speaks to Ananias he distinguishes between "the Gentiles" and "the sons of Israel" (Acts 9:15; cp. Luke 2:32; Acts 4:27).

This is made indisputably clear in Romans 16:25–26. There Paul points out that the "mystery" of Gentile salvation is hidden *only from the Gentiles*, not from the Old Testament prophets — for he defends his doctrine of the mystery by referring to "the scriptures of the prophets": "the revelation of the mystery, which was kept secret since the world began, but now is made manifest, and *by the scriptures of the prophets*, according to the commandment of the everlasting God, *made known to all nations* for the obedience of faith." Paul declares that the "mystery" is "now made manifest" to "*all* nations" — not just to Israel.

5. The new covenant unites Jew and Gentile into one body. Paul teaches us that Gentile Christians of the new covenant church are grafted into the stock of Israel (Rom 11:16–19). Indeed, we are united with the patriarchs of the old covenant, even while many ethnic Jews are cut out of the kingdom of God: "if some of the branches were broken off, and you, being a wild olive, were grafted in among them and became partaker with them of the rich root of the olive tree, do not be arrogant toward the branches; but if you are arrogant, remember that it is not you who supports the root, but the root supports you" (Rom 11:17–18). God's people are symbolized by one tree, not two.

Furthermore, Paul expressly declares that Christ's death wholly removes the wall of separation between Jew and Gentile, merging them into one: "He Himself is our peace, who made *both* groups into *one*, and *broke down the barrier of the dividing wall*" (Eph 2:14). Nothing hints that this great redemptive truth is temporary and will be removed later in the millennium, as per dispensational teaching.

In fact, the "cementing" agent in this union is the powerful blood of Christ: "But now in Christ Jesus you who formerly were far off have been brought near by the blood of Christ" (Eph 2:13). Consequently, he was "abolishing [*not* temporarily halting] in His flesh the enmity" that separated Jew and Gentile (Eph 2:15). This comports well with what Christ teaches when he presents himself as the Good Shepherd in John 10:16: "And I have *other sheep* [Gentiles] which are not of this fold; I must bring them also, and they shall hear My voice; and they shall become *one flock* with one shepherd."

Dispensationalism demands two groups and thus attempts to repair the barrier wall that Christ broke down as they make two people out of those whom Christ has made one. Whereas, the more biblical position would be to affirm: "What God has joined together, let no man separate."

6. The new covenant church is called Abraham's seed. Israel's biological descent from Abraham was a source of great Jewish pride. God is often called in Scripture "the God of Abraham."[4] Because he is "the God of Abraham" the Jews expected blessings in terms of their Abrahamic descent.[5] Yet in the new covenant, *Gentile* Christians are called the children of Abraham.

We see this in Galatians where Paul writes: "therefore, be sure that it is those who are of faith who are sons of Abraham. And the Scripture, foreseeing that God would justify the Gentiles by faith, preached the gospel beforehand to Abraham, saying, 'All the nations shall be blessed in you'"(Gal 3:7–8). Then a few verses later he forthrightly declares: "if you belong to Christ, then you are Abraham's offspring, heirs according to promise" (Gal 3:29).

7. The new covenant church sees old covenant Israel as their "fathers." Following up on the redemptive truth regarding our being children of Abraham, we discover also that new covenant Gentile Christians call Abraham "our father" (Rom 4:16). Paul can even call the old covenant patriarchs "our fathers" (1 Cor 10:1), clearly evincing a spiritual relationship uniting the new covenant people with the old covenant people, related as a seed to its fruit.

8. The new covenant church is given Jewish titles and descriptions. Scripture frequently applies old covenant terms to new covenant citizens: we are the "the circumcision" (Rom 2:28–29; Phil 3:3; Col 2:11; cp. Gen 17:13; Acts 7:8), "a royal priesthood," (Rom 15:16; 1 Pet 2:9; Rev 1:6; 5:10; cp.

---

[4] Gen 28:13; 31:42, 53; Exo 3:6, 15–16; 4:5; 1 Kgs 18:36; 1 Chron 29:18; 2 Chron 30:6; Psa 47:9; Matt 22:32; Mark 12:36; Luke 20:37; Acts 3:13; 7:32.

[5] Matt 3:9; 8:11; Luke 3:8; 13:16, 28; 16:23–30; 19:9; John 8:39, 53; Rom 11:1; 2 Cor 11:22.

Exo 19:6), and the "temple of God" (1 Cor 3:16–17; 6:19; 2 Cor 1:16; Eph 2:21). These terms clearly reflect Israel's covenantal identity, but are applied to the new covenant people.

Peter piles up some these Old Testament designations and others to the church. He calls Christians: "a chosen generation, a royal priesthood, an holy nation" (1 Pet 2:9–10), which is based on Exodus 19:5–6 and Deuteronomy 7:6. He and Paul call Christians "a peculiar people" (1 Pet 2:10; Tit 2:14), which is a familiar Old Testament designation for Israel (Exo 19:5; Deut 14:2; 26:18; Psa 135:4).

9. The new covenant church is actually called "Israel." Dispensationalists strongly resist the application of "Israel" to the church, asserting that "the Scriptures never use the term Israel to refer to any but the natural descendants of Jacob."[6] But if according to the *New Scofield Reference Bible* Abraham can have Gentiles as his "spiritual seed,"[7] why may we not envision a *spiritual Israel*?

In fact, Paul applies the name "Israel" to Christians when he writes: "And as many as walk according to this rule, peace and mercy be upon them, and upon the Israel of God" (Gal 6:16). Here he is referring to Christians as "the Israel of God." In the Greek the "and " preceding "the Israel of God," functions epexegetically. That is, we should translate the verse "peace and mercy upon them, *that is,* upon the Israel of God." Thus, according to Paul "as many as walk according to this rule [Christian faith]" are the "Israel of God."

Dispensationalists see Galatians 6:16 as applying to Jewish converts to Christ, "who would not oppose the apostle's glorious message of salvation."[8] But such is surely not the case, for the following reasons. The entire epistle of Galatians opposes any claim to a special Jewish status or distinction: "For you are all sons of God through faith in Christ Jesus. For as many of you as were baptized into Christ have put on Christ. There is neither Jew nor Greek, there is neither slave nor free, there is neither male nor female; for you are all one in Christ Jesus" (Gal 3:26–28).

So here Paul declares that in the new covenant Christ does away with all ethnic distinctions. Why would he hold out a special word for Jewish

---

[6] Charles L. Feinberg, *Millennialism: The Two Major Views* (3rd ed. Chicago: Moody, 1980), 230. "The term *Israel* is nowhere used in the Scriptures for any but the physical descendants of Abraham." Pentecost, *Things to Come*, 127.

[7] *New Scofield Reference Bible*, 1223 (at Ro 9:6).

[8] *New Scofield Reference Bible*, 1223.

Christians as "the Israel of God," when he states immediately beforehand that we must not boast at all, save in the cross of Christ (Gal 6:14)? In fact, "in Christ Jesus neither circumcision nor uncircumcision avails anything, but a new creation" (Gal 6:15). Elsewhere, Paul can even speak of an uncircumcised Gentile as "a *Jew* who is one inwardly" whose "*circumcision* is that which is of the heart" (Rom 2:28–29).

10. The new covenant removes all ethnic distinctions. In several places Paul drives home the point that the days of ethnic distinction in God's kingdom are over with. "There is neither Jew nor Greek . . . for you are all one in Christ" (Gal 3:28). "There is neither Greek nor Jew, circumcision nor uncircumcision" (Col 3:11). "For there is no distinction between Jew and Greek; for the same Lord is Lord of all, abounding in riches for all who call upon Him" (Rom 10:12). This principle of "neither Jew nor Greek" explains why the Old Testament promises and prophecies can apply to Gentile Christians and the pan-ethnic new covenant church. It also explains why we should no re-impose ethnic distinctions in our doctrine of the church.

Conclusion

Old Testament Israel was long the special, singular people of God. Dispensationalism is built on the view that she remains God's special people and will one day come again to prominence in God's dealings with man. In fact, the system is firmly rooted in the notion that Israel and the church must remain distinct. We have seen, though, that the Old Testament expected the expansion of Israel and that the New Testament speaks repeatedly of that expansion in such a way that we may see that the church is the new Israel.

REVIEW QUESTIONS FOR DISCUSSION

These questions deal directly with the material in this chapter. The answers can be found in the chapter.
1. Why is Israel such an important feature in the Bible?
2. Explain two problems that arise because of the dispensational view of Israel as having a special future in God's plan.
3. State three arguments by Ryrie for keeping Israel distinct from the church.
4. Show how the Old Testament anticipates the expanding of God's people Israel.

5. Does the New Testament apply Old Testament prophecies of Israel to the church? Provide evidence for your answer.

6. Paul speaks of the church as a "mystery" in Ephesians 3:5–6. Does this imply that it was wholly unknown in Old Testament prophecy? Give reasons for your answer.

7. What verses show that the New Testament people are merged with Israel to form one entity. Explain their significance for the debate with dispensationalism.

8. What Jewish descriptions are applied to the New Testament church? How does this impact our understanding of Israel?

9. Is the church ever directly called by the name "Israel." Explain your answer.

10. Does the church recognize ethnic distinctions among God's people? How would such a distinguishing of his people be contrary to New Testament principles?

STRETCHING FURTHER

1. Is the Christian expected to support modern Israel due to Scriptural obligations?

2. Did you ever hold to a special, elevated distinction of Israel? What arguments changed your view?

3. Have you ever tried to present postmillennialism to a dispensationalist and have them object on the basis of their understanding of Israel and her special promises? Explain.

4. Do you know of other arguments against distinguishing Israel from the church?

5. What were some new ideas you learned from this chapter?

Chapter 10
THE REBUILT TEMPLE IN POSTMILLENNIALISM

In the literalist's approach to Scripture, several Old Testament prophecies seem to promise a rebuilding of the Jewish temple at some time still in our future. Among those passages are: Isaiah 56:7; 66:20–23; Jeremiah 33:18; Zechariah 14:16–21; Ezekiel 40–48; and Malachi 3:3–4.

Dispensationalists argue that Jews will return to their Land so that their Messiah can rule over an exalted Jewish kingdom. This will involve a re-established temple and a re-constituted sacrificial system. They believe that many Old Testament passages "predict the Millennial Temple as the center of world renewal and blessing, turning all the nations to Temple worship."[1] In fact, dispensationalists expect *two* future temples: one built during the seven year tribulation and the other during the millennium.[2]

John Walvoord freely admits that "most thoroughgoing students of premillennialism [i.e., dispensationalism] who evince understanding of the relation of literal interpretation to premillennial doctrine usually embrace the concept of a literal temple and literal sacrifices."[3] Anyone at all familiar with dispensationalism recognizes this fact, for it distinguishes dispensationalism from the other evangelical views.

Another leading dispensationalist theologian John C. Whitcomb puts it even more strongly when he states that: "consistent dispensationalism must teach the practice of animal sacrifices for a restored and regenerated Israel in the Millennium."[4] He adds later: "Israel will have the only

---

[1] Tim LaHaye and Ed Hindson, eds., *The Popular Encyclopedia of Bible Prophecy* (Eugene, Ore.: Harvest House, 2004), 373.

[2] LaHaye and Hindson, *Popular Encyclopedia*, 372–73; Mal Couch, ed., *Dictionary of Premillennial Theology Dictionary of Premillennial Theology* (Grand Rapids: Kregel, 1996), 404–05. John F. Walvoord, *Prophecy Knowledge Handbook* (Wheaton, Ill.: Victor, 1990), 199.

[3] John F. Walvoord, *The Millennial Kingdom* (Findlay, Ohio: Dunham), 1959. 315. See also: Thomas Ice and Randall Price, *Ready to Rebuild: Imminent Plan to Rebuild the Last Days Temple* (Eugene, Ore.: Harvest, 1992), 130ff.

[4] John C. Whitcomb, "Christ's Atonement and Animal Sacrifices" *Grace Theological Journal* 6:2 (1985):215.

sanctuary and priesthood in the world during the Millennial Kingdom; thus the temple courts and sacred areas will need to be very large to accommodate the vast number of priests and Levites."[5]

The fundamental passage undergirding this view is the famous extended description in Ezekiel 40–48. According to dispensationalists: "Ezekiel 40–48 not only indicates that there will be a temple in the Millennium, but also seems to indicate that sacrifices will be reinstituted in this temple as well."[6]

This doctrine is so patently erroneous — both theologically and exegetically — that some scholars call it the "Achilles' heel of the Dispensational system of interpretation."[7] Even dispensationalists recognize that "the future function of the millennial temple (Ezekiel 40–48) has long been problematic for dispensationalists."[8] Postmillennialism, on the other hand, can explain the prophecies of the rebuilt temple in a reasonable way that does not compromise the progress of redemption and the fulfillment of the sacrificial system in Christ.

But first let us consider:

The Dispensational View

In an important book on the topic, Walvoord presents the dispensational position on Ezekiel's millennial temple: "In the Millennium, apparently, sacrifices will also be offered, though somewhat different than those required under the Mosaic Law, but this time the sacrifices will be memorial, much as the Lord's Supper is a memorial in the Church Age for the death of Christ."[9]

---

[5] John C. Whitcomb in Tim LaHaye, ed., *Prophecy Study Bible* (Chattanooga: AMG, 2001), 979.

[6] Mark F. Rooker in Donald K. Campbell and Jeffrey L. Townsend, eds., *A Case for Premillennialism: A New Consensus* (Chicago: Moody, 1992), 131.

[7] O. T. Allis, *Prophecy and the Church* (Philadelphia: Presbyterian and Reformed, 1945), 248.

[8] Whitcomb, "Christ's Atonement," 201.

[9] Walvoord, *Prophecy Knowledge Handbook*, 202. Fellow dispensationalist Whitcomb disagrees that the sacrifices will be only memorial: "Future animal sacrifices will be 'efficacious' and 'expiatory' only in terms of the strict provision for ceremonial (and thus temporal) forgiveness within the theocracy of Israel." Whitcomb, "Christ's Atonement and Animal Sacrifices," 210. But Walvoord's view is the predominant view in popular dispensationalism, as is demonstrated by John L. Mitchell, "The Question of Millennial Sacrifices," *Bibliotheca Sacra* 110 (1953):

The argument for such a temple in the millennium is ultimately due to dispensationalism's extreme, literalistic hermeneutic. In fact, they vigorously press this point, as a matter of fundamental principle. They hold that allowing a symbolic interpretation of Ezekiel's prophecy is hermeneutically flawed in that it leaves "unanswered why such specific details were revealed" to Ezekiel.[10] Furthermore, Walvoord admits, "those who adopt the figurative interpretation have not agreed as to the meaning of this temple"[11] (as if differences of opinion were absent in dispensational discussions of this issue[12]). Here is his rationale for a rebuilt temple:

"Though it is objectionable to some to have animal sacrifices in the millennial scene, actually, they will be needed there because the very ideal circumstances in which millennial saints will live will tend to gloss over the awfulness of sin and the need for bloody sacrifice. The sacrifices offered will therefore be a reminder that only by the shedding of blood and, more specifically, the blood of Christ, can sin be taken away."[13]

Unfortunately, the popular dispensational perspective is fraught with debilitating problems.

The dispensationalist view is hermeneutically flawed

In the previous chapter we comment on the error of literalism as a basic hermeneutic. What is more, in Ezekiel 40ff we have divine *visions*.[14] This fact of a vision could easily militate against literalism, because Scripture often ideally conceptualizes spiritual truths when it presents them

---

248ff.

[10] Some historic premillennialists agree, as per Richard S. Hess: "It seems best to describe the time of the restored temple [of Eze 40–48] as millennial or as the millennium." Hess, "The Future Written in the Past," in Craig L. Blomberg and Sung Wook Chung, eds., *Case for Historic Premillennialism: An Alternative to "Left Behind" Eschatology* (rand Rapids: Baker, 2009), 34. 28–35.

[11] Walvoord, *Prophecy Knowledge Handbook*, 202. Cf. Don Stewart and Chuck Missler, *The Coming Temple: Center Stage for the Final Countdown* (Orange, Calif.: Dart, 1991), 227ff.

[12] Two prominent dispensationalists who deny a future temple are H. A. Ironside (*Expository Notes on Ezekiel the Prophet* [New York: Loizeaux, 1949], 284ff) and J. Sidlow Baxter, *Explore the Book* (Grand Rapids: Zondervan, 1960), 32ff).

[13] Walvoord, *Prophecy Knowledge Handbook*, 202

[14] Daniel I. Block, *The Book of Ezekiel, Chapters 25–48* (Grand Rapids: Eerdmans, 1998), 496.

in vision form. Indeed, spiritual truths would be impossible to present in a vision without resorting to symbolism. This is the same sort of vision occurring in earlier chapters in Ezekiel, where the prophet *frames spiritual truths as concrete realities*. See particularly Ezekiel 1–3 and 8–11 (note the distinction between a vision and direct revelation in Num 12:6).

In fact, we cannot literally interpret certain aspects of the temple vision: (1) The site of the temple is on a "very high mountain" (Eze 40:2), although Jerusalem has no "very high mountain." Jerusalem is slightly over 2000 feet high. (2) The river's source and flow is incredible — flowing from under the temple's threshold it becomes a great river (Eze 47:1–2). (3) The river's making the Dead Sea fresh and bringing life to all that it touches (Eze 47:6–12) is surely symbolism. (4) The Twelve Tribes receive exactly parallel-portioned tracts of land, which would be awkward in real geography (Eze 47:13ff).

Thus, the exegetical problems facing the dispensational view of future sacrifices are just too great. Even dispensationalist recognize this problem. For instance, the *New Scofield Reference Bible* (1967) notes of the *sin offering* sacrifices in Ezekiel 43:19: "the reference to sacrifices is not to be taken literally."[15] Here it makes a major concession to dispensationalism's critics, while breeching one of their fundamental principles, literalism.

Dispensationalists argue that the particular details in Ezekiel's temple vision militate against a symbolic portrayal. Nevertheless, symbolic portrayal is quite common in Ezekiel.[16]

Consider the following: When Isaiah speaks of the king of Tyre, he does so in a few verses in brief, general terms (Isa 23:1–17). But when Ezekiel speaks of him, he provides many details in three chapters dealing with that king's greatness and fall (Eze 26–28). Ezekiel even presents the king of Tyre himself as if he had been *perfect* (Eze 28:12) and *blameless* (Eze 28:15); and as if he had actually lived in the Garden of Eden (Eze 28:13). Note that God speaks to Ezekiel *about the king of Tyre*: "Son of man, take up a lamentation over the king of Tyre, and say to him. . ." (Eze 28:12). Yet his description of the king is not literal, but symbolic.

The special details of the Ezekiel's temple vision flow from Ezekiel's being a priest (Eze 1:3) and his concern is to characterize Israel's sin as

---

[15] *New Scofield Reference Bible* (Oxford: University Press, 1967), 888, note 1.
[16] See: Patrick Fairbairn, *An Exposition of Ezekiel* (Minneapolis, Minn.: Klock & Klock, rep. 1979 [1851]), 431–450.

centering in the temple (Eze 8–11). Thus, he symbolically portrays the future glory as if it involved a literal temple. We must note that even Moses' tabernacle and Solomon's temple are material symbols of heavenly and spiritual truths that impact their construction. So why should not a vision allow for such detail in portraying spiritual truths? The spiritual truth is more glorious than the physical building.

Furthermore, John's vision of the New Jerusalem obviously reflects back in some ways upon Ezekiel's vision. John seems to adapt Ezekiel's vision as portraying God's kingdom in history.[17] But John's is manifestly a symbolic portrayal, for the city's size is a 1,500 mile cube (Rev 21:16). This would cause the top of the city to extend more than 1300 miles beyond the orbit of the International Space Station (ISS), which orbits at 190 miles above the earth.

Like John's vision of the new Jerusalem, Ezekiel's vision of the temple is almost certainly an ideal symbol, not a prophecy of a literal temple. This becomes *actually* certainly when we consider the final, New Testament revelation, which leads to my next objection against a rebuilt temple.

The dispensational view is redemptively retrogressive

The temple, priesthood, and sacrifices were all part of the typological, old covenant order which permanently ended with the coming of the final new covenant. As postmillennialist David Brown complained over a century ago: Such a position is guilty of "Judaizing our Christianity, instead of Christianizing the adherents of Judaism."[18]

If we interpret Ezekiel's temple vision literally it would reimpose *circumcision* and displace baptism: "No foreigner, uncircumcised in heart or uncircumcised in flesh, shall enter My sanctuary, including any foreigner who is among the children of Israel" (Eze 44:9). This re-establishes what the New Testament asserts is forever disestablished.[19] Christ permanently removes the circumcision-based, separating-partition between Jew and

---

[17] Beasley-Murray, "Ezekiel," in Donald Guthrie and J. A. Motyer, eds., *The Eerdmans Bible Commentary* (3d. ed.: Grand Rapids: Eerdmans, 1970), 684. Most Revelation commentators see Ezekiel's immense influence on Revelation.

[18] David Brown, *Christ's Second Coming: Will It Be Premillennial?* (Edmonton, Alb.: Still Waters Revival, rep. 1990 [1882]), 352.

[19] Acts 15; Rom 2:26–29; 4:9–12; 1 Cor 7:18–19; Gal 5:2–6; 6:12–15; Phil 3:3; Col 2:11; 3:11.

Gentile (Eph 2:11–21). The "true circumcision" are those who worship Christ in the Spirit (Phil 3:3), for "in Christ Jesus neither circumcision nor uncircumcision means anything" (Gal 5:6; Col 2:11).

A literalistic approach to Ezekiel's vision would re-institute *redemptive* sacrifices, despite the new covenant's fulfilling and removing them (John 4:20–24; Heb 7:27; 8:13; 9:26; 10:1–14). It re-institutes "the burnt offering, the sin offering, and the trespass offering" (Eze 40:39; cf. 43:21), though Christ takes these away (Heb 10:5, 9, 18). Why would the Lord have us return again to the "weak and beggarly elements" of the ceremonial law (Gal 4:9)?

John 4:21 anticipates the removing of the temple order: "The hour is coming when you will neither on this mountain, nor in Jerusalem, worship the Father." Hebrews 8:13 does as well: "When He said, 'A new covenant,' He has made the first obsolete. But whatever is becoming obsolete and growing old is ready to disappear." Various other Old Testament prophecies transcend the Mosaic pattern of worship in the temple environs (Isa 19:19; Jer 3:16; Zec 14:21; Mal 1:11). Which shall we follow? Biblical references that transcend a central, temple-based worship, or dispensational proponents who want to reintroduce it?

Obviously, we are dealing with symbolic language. When properly interpreted no contradiction exists between the two types of references. Historic premillennialists recognize the problem but moan: "I cannot easily harmonize the two streams of teaching in the New Testament," nevertheless "if we cannot flatten out all the bumps in this picture, I will not worry."[20] But the bumps need flattening because of the final revelation of God in the New Testament. We do not need bumps when Jesus sends us into the highways to invite men into the kingdom (Matt 22:9; Luke 14:23). Indeed, John the Baptist's ministry of introducing Christ was to make "the rough roads smooth" (Luke 3:5).

Significantly, the text provides us with absolutely *no hint* that these sacrifices will be "memorial," as per the great majority of dispensationalists (and contrary, by the way, to their literalism). Dispensationalist Whitcomb writes: "Ezekiel, however, does not say that animals will be offered for a 'memorial' of Messiah's death. Rather, they will be for 'atonement' (45:15, 17, 20; cf. 43:20, 26)."[21] He is correct. Ezekiel's sacri-

---

[20] Richard S. Hess in Blomberg and Chung, *A Case for Historic Premillennialism*, 35.

[21] Whitcomb, "Christ's Atonement," 211.

fices are those Moses establishes in the Levitical system, if *literally* conceived (see the reference to the "sons of Levi" in Eze 40:46; cp. Eze 43:19; 44:10, 15).

The Old Testament clearly speaks of their legal function as *actually making reconciliation*. In fact, in Ezekiel 45:15, 17, 20 the sacrifices that will be offered in the (supposed) future temple are specifically said to "make reconciliation" or "atonement." They are *not* memorials. The Hebrew phraseology used here — the piel (intensive) form of *kaphar* — is identical to that which Moses uses in Leviticus and Numbers where the sacrifices did make atonement.[22]

But now we must ask Walvoord: How could the "millennial scene" require bloody sacrifices "because the very ideal circumstances in which millennial saints will live will tend to gloss over the awfulness of sin and the need for bloody sacrifice"? This is a surprising concern!

Does this mean that the universal prevalence of the righteous knowledge of God (Isa 11:9) under the direct administration of Christ in the dispensationalist millennium "glosses over the awfulness of sin"? Would not such universal, deeply rooted righteousness make sin all the more heinous and conspicuous? And does not the Lord want us *today* deeply to recognize the awfulness of sin? Why then did not the sacrificial system continue in the *present*? Do not the words in the administration of the Lord's Supper point to the awful fact of sin — *without animal sacrifices* (1 Cor 11:23–32)?

The Postmillennial View

To understand the significance of Ezekiel's temple vision, we must keep in mind the conceptual idea which the temple structure and services embody. In essence the temple itself is a symbol: it symbolizes the *covenantal relationship* of God with his people — emphasizing his special presence among them.

The heart of the covenant appears in the frequently repeated promise: "I will be your God, you will be My people."[23] Consequently, the temple is the special place where God dwells among his people (1 Kgs 6:12–13; Jer 7:4–7), as he did in the temple's forerunner, the tabernacle

---

[22] Lev 6:30; 8:15; 16:6, 11, 24, 30; Nu 5:8; 15:28; 29:5.
[23] See: Gen 17:7; Exo 5:2; 6:7; 29:45; Lev 11:45; 26:12,45; Deut 4:20; 7:9; 29:14–15; 2 Sam 7:24; Ps 105:9; Isa 43:6; Jer 24:7; 31:33; 32:38; Eze 11:20; 34:24; 36:28; 37:23; Hos 1:10; Zec 8:8; 13:9; 2 Cor 6:18; Rev 21:3, 7.

(Exo 29:42; 25:22; 30:36). God's glory is especially present there in his sanctuary (1 Kgs 8:11; 2 Chron 7:1–2), even though no temple could contain his immense being (1 Kgs 8:27; Isa 66:1; Jer 23:24).

This idea of God's special presence clearly relates to Ezekiel's temple vision in Ezekiel 48:35. There even the city where the temple is located is characterized by the special presence of God: "The name of the city from that day shall be: The Lord is There." Thus, postmillennialism sees Ezekiel's visionary temple as symbolizing God's glorious presence in Christ's kingdom, which comes in the final, new covenant era. And this is so because when further defined, the temple symbolized Christ himself.

We must recognize that Ezekiel is a very symbolic work, perhaps second only to Revelation in all the Bible. For instance, his vision of the valley of dry bones coming together and standing on their feet as a great army (Eze 37:1–10), symbolizes the restoration of his people from a period of judgment. His vision of the water flowing from the temple and becoming a great river that flows into the sea (Eze 47:1–12), symbolizes the life-giving Spirit of God flowing into all the world. In Ezekiel 40–44 we find God's presence among his people gloriously displayed as new, huge temple. As Edmund Clowney notes:

> "Ezekiel's vision of the new temple is part of this prophetic pattern of a restoration so total that it sublimates the ceremonial structure in glory. Ezekiel's restoration returns David to the throne, and sees a temple that is a sanctuary of Paradise, where the river of life flows from God's throne past trees whose leaves are for the healing of the nations."[24]

Christ is God's true presence

John's Gospel opens with the statement that "in the beginning was the Word, and the Word was with God, and the Word was God" (John 1:1). It then goes on to say that "the Word became flesh, and dwelt among us, and we saw His glory, glory as of the only begotten from the Father, full of grace and truth" (John 1:14; cf. John 1:1; 1 John 1:1–3). In Jesus, God dwelled among us.

---

[24] Edmund P. Clowney, "The Final Temple," *Westminster Theological Journal*, 35.2 (1973):106. The insights presented below largely derive from Clowney's study.

Jesus himself teaches his disciples that whoever sees him sees the Father (John 14:9). This is because "in Him dwells all the fullness of the Godhead bodily" (Col 2:9). He even transfigures before his disciples, gloriously displaying his true identity within (Matt 17:1–8; Mark 9:2–8).

Thomas initially doubted Christ's resurrection, since he was not with the other disciples who saw him (John 20:24–25). When he finally did see the resurrected Lord he recognized that he was God in the flesh, for Thomas "answered and said to Him, 'My Lord and my God!'" (John 20:28).

Because of his glorious identity as God, in Christ God is with us. And because of this:

Christ is the true temple

As we shall see, the New Testament writers present Christ as the new temple. He stands as the glorious realization of the temple's very meaning and purpose. Thus, he justly claims to be *greater than the temple* (Matt 12:6) in that he is its fulfillment.

We can see this by returning once again to John 1:14, but noticing a particular point more closely. There Christ's first-century ministry is spoken of as his coming to "tabernacle" among his people: "the Word became flesh, and dwelt [Gk.: *eskēnōsen*, "tabernacled"] among us" (John 1:14; cf. John 1:1; 1 John 1:1–3). The noun form of this Greek word is *skēnē*, which is used of the Old Testament tabernacle (Acts 7:44; Heb 8:5; 9:2–21; 13:10). This noun appears very frequently in the Greek version of the Old Testament as the word for the "tabernacle" (e.g., Exo 26:1–35; 27:9; 29:5–11, 30, 42ff).

When Jesus is born, shepherds are quite appropriately the first to visit him — shepherds from out in the fields keeping *sacrificial sheep* destined for the temple.[25] When his parents present him forty days later in the temple, Simeon praises him as the "glory of Your people Israel" (Luke 2:32) — language reflecting God's Shekinah glory in the tabernacle/temple (Exo 40:34, 35; 1 Sam 4:21–22).

Consequently, as the Lord's public ministry opens, John the Baptist declares that Jesus is the sacrificial "Lamb of God" — destined for temple service as he takes away sin (John 1:29). Christ himself even stands in the shadow of the earthly temple and informs Jerusalem of a glorious truth:

---

[25] William Hendriksen, *Exposition of the Gospel according to Luke* (Grand Rapids: Baker, 1978), 150. The presence of shepherds in the fields in winter months indicates the tending of sacrificial sheep.

"Destroy this temple, and in three days I will raise it up" — by which "He was speaking of the temple of His body" (John 2:19, 21), a temple "not made with hands" (Mark 14:58).

The Lord applies to himself a number of temple images as he presents himself as its fulfillment. He offers himself to men as the heavenly manna, which was once housed in the Ark of the Covenant in the temple (1 Kgs 6:19; 2 Chron. 35:3), as we see in John 6:49–58 (cp. Rev 2:17; cf. Exo 16:33–34; Heb 9:4). He provides to believers the living water pictured in Ezekiel's temple (Eze 47:1–12; cp. Joel 3:18; Zech 14:8). We see this in John 4:10–15; 7:38–39.

Edmund Clowney well notes in this regard that "we must recognize that this is not spiritualization in our usual sense of the word, but the very opposite. In Christ is *realization*. It is not so much that Christ fulfills what the temple means; rather Christ is the meaning for which the temple existed."[26]

Therefore, when he speaks of the temple's absolute destruction in AD 70, he does not suggest any God-endorsed rebuilding (Matt 24). Nor does he speak of the temple *mount*'s return to holy status (John 4:21–24). He even tells the corrupt Jews that it is no longer God's house (Matt 21:13; Luke 2:49), but "your house" (Matt 23:38).

Christ's body as the temple

By God's grace, Christ's people are in mystical union with him, as Paul repeatedly declares.[27] Because of this we are called his "body" (Rom 12:5; 1 Cor 12:27; Eph 4:12). Due to our union with him we are also designated a "temple" (1 Cor 3:16–17; 6:19; 2 Cor 6:16; Eph 2:19–20; 1 Pet 2:5–9).

Thus, Old Testament prophecies regarding the temple's rebuilding (when not referring to Zerubbabel's Old Testament temple, Ezra 5:2; Zech 4:9) speak of Christ and his building his church (Matt 16:18; cf. Zec 6:12–13). He himself is the foundation and cornerstone upon which we are built (Luke 20:17; 1 Cor 3:11, 16–17; Eph 2:20). Extending the temple metaphor, as his people we are also *priests* (Rom 15:16; 1 Pet 2:5, 9; Rev

---

[26] Clowney, "The Final Temple," 119.
[27] Rom 3:24; 6:11, 23; 8:1; 9:1; 12:5; 15:17; 16:3, 7, 9,10; 1 Cor 1:2, 30; 3:1; 4:10, 15, 17; 15:18, 19, 22, 31; 16:24; 2 Cor 1:21; 2:14, 17; 3:14; 5:17, 19; 11:3; 12:2, 19; Gal 1:22; 2:4, 16; 3:14, 17, 26, 28; 5:6; 6:15; Eph 1:1, 3, 10, 12, 20; 2:6, 7, 10, 13; 3:11; 4:32; Phil 1:1, 13; 2:1, 5; 3:3, 9, 14; 4:21; Col 1:2, 4, 28; 2:5; 1 Thess 2:14; 4:16; 5:18; 1 Tim 1:14; 2:7; 3:13; 2 Tim 1:1, 9, 13; 2:1, 10; 3:12, 15.

1:6) who offer our bodies as *living sacrifices* (Rom 12:1–2) and our service as acceptable *sweet smell offerings* (2 Cor 2:14–16; Phil 4:18; Heb 13:15–16; 1 Pet 2:5).

As more people are converted by his grace, his new covenant temple grows stone-by-stone (Eph 2:21; 4:12, 16; 1 Pet 2:5, 9). Consequently, as a master builder Paul labors in that temple-building project (1 Cor 3:9–17). In fact, through a series of Old Testament temple and ritual allusions, Paul points to *the new temple of God*:

"And what agreement has the temple of God with idols? For you are the temple of the living God. As God has said: 'I will dwell in them and walk among them. I will be their God, and they shall be My people.' Therefore 'Come out from among them and be separate, says the Lord. Do not touch what is unclean, and I will receive you. I will be a Father to you, and you shall be My sons and daughters, says the Lord Almighty.' Therefore, having these promises, beloved, let us cleanse ourselves from all filthiness of the flesh and spirit, perfecting holiness in the fear of God." (2 Cor 6:16–7:1)

John Taylor distills the basic ideas in Ezekiel's complex temple vision: (1) The building's immaculate symmetry portrays the perfection of God's plan for his people. (2) The meticulous detail of the rites indicates the centrality of worship in the new covenant era. (3) The focus on the temple points to God's abiding presence with his redeemed community. (4) The waters of life flowing from the temple express Holy Spirit's life-giving operation in the new age. (5) The careful allocation of levitical duties and land apportionment speak of the duties and privileges of God's people in the future.[28]

Conclusion

A true new covenant theology recognizes the finished work of Christ as rendering any physical temple and sacrificial service obsolete (Heb 10:4–18). The rebuilt temple that the Bible anticipates is the continuing building of the spiritual temple of God, the church of Jesus Christ, the body of Christ To propose a future, physical temple is to deny the final fulfillment of the temple in Christ.

---

[28] John B. Taylor, *Ezekiel: An Introduction and Commentary* (TOTC) (Downer's Grove, Ill.: InterVarsity Press, 1969), 253–354.

This is why the writer of Hebrews insists: "He said, 'Behold, I have come to do Your will.' He takes away the first in order to establish the second. By this will we have been sanctified through the offering of the body of Jesus Christ once for all" (Heb 10:9–10).

REVIEW QUESTIONS FOR DISCUSSION

These questions deal directly with the material in this chapter. The answers can be found in the chapter.

1. What are two ways dispensationalists understand the call to a renewed sacrificial system in the millennium? That is, what are the two distinct ways they understand their function at that time?
2. What are some problems with literally interpreting Ezekiel's grand vision of the rebuilt temple? Can you think of others?
3. John's Revelation apparently shows an influence from Ezekiel's temple vision. But what are some features of John's vision of the new Jerusalem that suggest it is not a literal city?
4. What are some elements in Ezekiel's vision that show the danger of trying to interpret his temple vision literally? That is, what are some redemptively retrogressive problems that arise in such an approach to the vision?
5. Where does the New Testament suggest the need for a physical temple is past?
6. Dispensationalist John Walvoord sees the renewed sacrifices in the millennium as necessary for insuring that saints not gloss over sin. What are some problems with this understanding? Can you think of some additional problems not mentioned in our chapter?
7. What is the very essence of the Old Testament temple's significance for old covenant Israel? This is a key to understanding the function of the temple and its eventual removal.
8. How does Christ represent the presence of God among his people? How does this impact the question of the need for a rebuilt temple?
9. The New Testament speaks of the building of a temple. To what does it refer? Explain your answer and provide biblical texts in support of it.
10. What are some ways by which a non-dispensationalist can explain Ezekiel's temple complex?

STRETCHING FURTHER

1. Have you ever read Christian articles or advertisements calling for funds to help rebuild the temple? Where? What did you think of that call at the time?
2. Do you have friends (or family members) who are strongly committed to dispensationalism and the rebuilt temple? Are they open to discussion of the matter? Is this a matter that can get emotional?
3. How significant do you think a rebuilt temple is for dispensationalism? Would you think the system absolutely must require such?
4. Besides those points mentioned in this chapter, can you think of other reasons that a rebuilt physical temple is contrary to Scripture and to redemptive history.
5. What were some new ideas you learned from this chapter?

Chapter 11
PROPHETIC TIME-FRAMES IN POSTMILLENNIALISM

Eschatology brings history to its God-ordained conclusion. Consequently, time-frames are important issues in understanding biblical prophecy. We will look at a few important temporal issues to assist us in our study of eschatology. We will begin with a temporal concern that many do not even consider in prophetic studies: gradualism in the outworking of God's actions in history.

Gradualism in Prophecy

Throughout Scripture the principle of gradualism has been the method of God and the experience of God's people. We will be showing that if we are to properly understand Scripture's eschatological victory, we must recognize this important redemptive-historical *method* of divine operation. In short, this principle expects the kingdom's gradual unfolding and incremental expansion over time.

Contrary to postmillennialism, though, the dispensational and premillennial views operate on the basis of the principle of *catastrophism*. As premillennialist theologian Millard Erickson puts it: "Whereas the postmillennialist thinks that the millennium is being introduced gradually, perhaps almost imperceptibly, the premillennialist envisions a sudden, cataclysmic event."[1] Dispensationalists believe that at Christ's sudden second advent "he will depose the earthly rulers and will begin His millennial reign."[2] In their theological systems Christ's kingdom with all of its attendant glory will invade history as a great catastrophe, being suddenly imposed on a recalcitrant world in relatively brief period of time.

God's ways and gradualism
A quick survey of some key concepts in Scripture suggests that gradualism is a common divine method of operation in history. Consider five clear samples:

---

[1] Millard J. Erickson, *Christian Theology* (Grand Rapids: Baker, 1998), 1217.
[2] Bobby Hayes, "Premillennialism" in Mal Couch, ed., *Dictionary of Premillennial Theology* (Grand Rapids: Kregel, 1996), 311.

Creation. Even God's creating the universe proceeds upon a gradualistic principle — an accelerated gradualism, to be sure, but gradualism nonetheless. God creates the world out of nothing, but he does not create it as a complete system by one divine command — though he could easily have done so. He employs a series of successive divine commands that gradually unfold over a period of six days (Gen 1; Exo 20:11). He apparently does this to establish a pattern for man's work and rest cycle (Exo 20:9; 31:17).

Dominion. Though God places Adam in the Garden of Eden with a command to cultivate the soil there (Gen 2:15), he expects him to begin working out the implications of the Cultural Mandate into *all the world* (Gen 1:26–28). Sung W. Chung notes that "Adam's rule was anticipated to be extended to the entire creation beyond the boundary of the garden of Eden."[3] This obviously requires a long, slow process.

This gradualistic dominion process is re-issued in the great commission which anticipates a long process: "Go therefore and make disciples of all the nations, baptizing them in the name of the Father and the Son and the Holy Spirit, teaching them to observe all that I commanded you; and lo, I am with you always, even to the end of the age" (Matt 28:19–20).

Redemption. God promises redemption just after sin enters into the human race in Eden (Gen 3:15). Yet its accomplishment follows thousands of years after Adam, when Christ (the ultimate seed of the woman) finally comes "in the fulness of time" (Gal 4:4; Eph 1:10). He even teaches while on the earth in the first century: "Truly I say to you that many prophets and righteous men desired to see what you see, and did not see it, and to hear what you hear, and did not hear it" (Matt 13:17).

Revelation. Rather than giving his total special revelation all at once, God gradually unfolds his word to men over a period of 1,500 years (Heb 1:1, 2; 1Pe 1:10–12). Interestingly, God even informs Israel that he teaches them knowledge of his will little-by-little: "For He says, 'Order on order, order on order, / Line on line, line on line, / A little here, a little there'" (Isa 28:10). Jesus instructs his disciples regarding God's final revelation: "I have many more things to say to you, but you cannot bear them now. But when He, the Spirit of truth, comes, He will guide you into all the truth; for He will not speak on His own initiative, but whatever He

---

[3] Craig L. Blomberg and Sung Wook Chung, eds., *Case for Historic Premillennialism: An Alternative to "Left Behind" Eschatology* (Grand Rapids: Baker, 2009), 139.

hears, He will speak; and He will disclose to you what is to come" (John 16:12–13).

Sanctification. Even in our salvation we see the gradualistic principle operation. Though justification is a once-for-all act (Rom 4:2–3; 5:1), it gives rise to sanctification, which comes by process over time (1Pe 2:2). Paul calls us to 'work out your salvation with fear and trembling; for it is God who is at work in you, both to will and to work for His good pleasure" (Phil 2:12b–13).

The kingdom and gradualism

Now we must note that God's redemptive kingdom also develops gradually. It incrementally unfolds through history, progressing from small, imperceptible beginnings to a glorious, dominant, worldwide conclusion. We will survey several relevant passages illustrating this important principle.

An historical indicator of kingdom gradualism appears in the Promised Land's conquest. In Deuteronomy 7:22 we read: "And the Lord your God will clear away these nations before you little by little; you will not be able to put an end to them quickly, lest the wild beasts grow too numerous for you." Here Moses specifically informs Israel that gradual conquest is for her good, allowing her people to conquer where they could secure and maintain control.

In Daniel 2:31–45 Christ's kingdom comes down to earth as a stone smiting the world kingdom, which exists under a fourth imperial rule. As we read through the passage we learn that the kingdom grows to become a great mountain in the earth:

> "You watched while a stone was cut out without hands, which struck the image on its feet of iron and clay, and broke them in pieces . . . . And the *stone* that struck the image *became a great mountain* and filled the whole earth. And in the days of these kings the God of heaven will set up a kingdom which shall never be destroyed; and the kingdom shall not be left to other people; it shall break in pieces and consume all these kingdoms, and it shall stand forever." (Dan 2:34–35, 44)

In this imagery we have both linear continuity over time and upward development to victory: the stone *grows* to become a "great mountain." We also witness struggle and resistance: the stone smashes the image. Finally, we rejoice in its fortunes: the God-defying image is thoroughly crushed.

In Ezekiel 17:22–24 God promises to establish the kingdom as a small "sprig from the lofty top of the cedar." Then he will nurture it until it becomes "a stately cedar." Ultimately, it will produce great boughs so that "birds of every kind will nest under it." This growth is certain for "I am the LORD; I have spoken, and I will perform it."

In Ezekiel 47:1–9 redemption gradually flows from God's temple as an ever-deepening stream. The waters of life trickle from under the altar, first "to the ankles" (Eze 47:3), then they flow gradually deeper to the knees (Eze 47:4a), then deeper still to the loins (Eze 47:4b), until the stream finally becomes "a river that I could not ford" (Eze 47:5). This is the river of life (Eze 47:9). In fact, in John 7:38 Christ presents himself as fulfilling this prophecy.[4]

This water-from-the-altar is quite consistent with Christ's presenting himself as the true temple (John 2:19–21). In John 7:38 we read: "He who believes in Me, as the Scripture has said, out of his heart will flow rivers of living water." At Pentecost in Acts 2 the torrential flow of the living water begins in earnest (Acts 2:33).

In Matthew 13 the Kingdom Parables speak of the kingdom's growing increase in external size and transformational influence (see chapter 4 above). Matthew 13:3–9 portrays the kingdom as scattered seed that gradually grows to bear abundant fruit. Matthew 13:31–33 likens the kingdom's external growth to a mustard seed which becomes a great plant and its internal penetration working like a little leaven expanding through three bushels of meal. I

In Mark 4 God's kingdom begins as mere seed (Mark 4:26). But then it puts forth the blade, then the head, the mature grain (Mark 4:27–28).

In Romans and 1 John the apostles see the kingdom light as already shining, ready to dispel the darkness:

> "The night is almost gone, and the day is at hand. Let us therefore lay aside the deeds of darkness and put on the armor of light." (Rom 13:12)

---

[4] John Jefferson Davis, *Christ's Victorious Reign: Postmillennialism Reconsidered* (Grand Rapids: Baker, 1986), 40 and David E. Holwerda, *Jesus and Israel: One Covenant or Two?* (Grand Rapids: Zondervan, 1995), 74–79. For a helpful treatment of John 7:38, see: William Hendriksen, *Exposition of the Gospel according to John* (Grand Rapids: Baker, 1953), 21–26.

"On the other hand, I am writing a new commandment to you, which is true in Him and in you, because the darkness is passing away, and the true light is already shining." (1 John 2:8)

Satan will not be able to thwart the kingdom's progress and growth, for the "gates of Hades will not be able to prevail against it" (Matt 16:18). Though slow, it will advance in God's good time.

The kingdom and gradual dominance

Some mistakenly suppose that postmillennial optimism implies either the ultimate salvation of all people that will ever live (final universalism) or at least the salvation of all people living at some future time in earth history (temporal universalism).

Kim Riddlebarger, for instance, writes against postmillennialism: "Although the kingdom advances throughout this age, the final eschatological victory is won by Jesus Christ himself at his second coming (1 Cor 15:54). Not before." And of certain negative verses, he comments that they "all speak of the present spiritual kingdom as finally consummated in 'the age to come' but not before."[5]

Robert Reymond believes regarding the postmillennial vision that "the world of mankind of necessity must be brought eventually to a state of virtual moral perfection — the major contention of postmillennialism . . . a representation of world conditions at the time of Christ's return which amillennialists reject."[6]

But postmillennialism does *not* claim that full and absolute eschatological victory comes before Christ returns. We are neither universalists nor perfectionists. We do, however, believe that because of the kingdom's long-term expansion "the number finally of the lost in comparison with the whole number of the saved will be very inconsiderable."[7] And even that the redeemed "shall embrace the immensely greater part of the human race"[8]; that "ultimately the vast majority of the whole mass of

---

[5] Kim Riddlebarger, *A Case for Amillennialism: Understanding the End Times* (Grand Rapids: Baker, 2003), 97, 99.

[6] Robert L. Reymond, *A New Systematic Theology of the Christian Faith* (Nashville: Thomas Nelson, 1998), 1036.

[7] Charles Hodge, *Systematic Theology* (Grand Rapids: Eerdmans, rep. 1973), 3:879–80.

[8] Benjamin B. Warfield, *Biblical and Theological Studies* (Philadelphia: Presbyterian and Reformed, rep. 1952), 349.

humanity, including all generations, will be actually redeemed by Christ."[9] Though quite optimistic, none of these statements is universalistic.

Nor do we expect at any given point in history that *all* men will be born-again Christians. David Brown comments: "Have we not evidence that *during* that bright period the world's subjection to the scepter of Christ will not be quite absolute?"[10] Campbell writes that the phrase "Christianized world" certainly "does not mean that every living person will then be a Christian, or that every Christian will be a perfect Christian. It does surely mean that the righteous rule and authority of Christ the King will be recognized over all the earth."[11]

Boettner observes only that "evil in all its many forms eventually will be reduced to negligible proportions, that Christian principles will be the rule, not the exception, and that Christ will return to a truly Christianized world."[12]

The postmillennial kingdom's growth will be enormous, but will not entail an each-and-every universalism. Though clearly expecting Christ's dominion throughout the world, Scripture nevertheless teaches that even at the very height of kingdom progress, a minority of the human race will not be converted to Christ. Evidence for this exists in the events associated with Christ's return, which include a brief rebellion, as indicated in 2 Thessalonians 1:7–10 and Revelation 20:7–9. In fact, the Lord himself expressly warns that we must always expect tares in the wheat field (Matt 13:39–43).

Some Bible exegetes suggest that Isaiah 19:18 may imply something on the order of a five-to-one ratio for Christians over non-Christians at the height of the millennial glory[13]: "in that day five cities in the land of

---

[9] Robert L. Dabney, *Lectures in Systematic Theology* (Grand Rapids: Zondervan, 1973 [rep. 1878]), 525.

[10] David Brown, *Christ's Second Coming: Will It Be Premillennial?* (Edmondton, AB: Still Waters Revival, 1882 (rep. 1990), 145.

[11] Roderick Campbell, *Israel and the New Covenant* (Tyler, Tex.: Geneva Divinity School, 1954 [rep. n.d.]), 298.

[12] Loraine Boettner, *The Millennium* (Philadelphia: Presbyterian and Reformed, 1957), 14.

[13] Alexander holds this view and notes it was Calvin's position, J. A. Alexander, *Commentary on the Prophecies of Isaiah* (Grand Rapids: Zondervan, rep. 1977 [1875]), 1:355–356. Matthew Henry leans to this interpretation. Matthew Henry, *Matthew Henry's Commentary on the Whole Bible* (Old Tappan, N. J., Revell, rep. n.d.), 4:108.

Egypt will speak the language of Canaan and swear by the LORD of hosts; one will be called the City of Destruction." To "speak the language" of God's people seems to indicate salvation. Language plays an important role in Scripture: if we hear the language of God's people, this evidences his favor (Isa 19:18; 57:19; Zeph 3:9); if not, it symbolizes his curse (Deut 28:49; Psa 81:5; 114:1; Jer 5:15; Eze 3:5–6).[14]

The progress of redemption not only grows slowly, though with occasional spurts, such as at the original Pentecost, at the Reformation, and during the Great Awakening. But it oftentimes develops sporadically, undergoing both ups-and-downs. Postmillennialists deny "that this current age will be a time of *steady* and upward growth."[15]

The historical progress of Christ's redemptive kingdom is often intermittent, even involving eras of divine pruning (John 15:5–6) in anticipation of the final harvest. Such pruning is certainly true of Israel of the Old Testament (Isa 6:9–13). At one point God offers to do away with Israel and establish a new people from out of Moses himself (Exo 32:10). Of course, by the new covenant era, this has long been Israel's experience (Matt 3:9–12; Rom 11:3, 16–24). Pruning can leave a region, once strongly influenced by Christianity, wholly without a Christian witness — for a time.

The kingdom is characterized by its living nature: it is like seed that is planted then grows and produces other seed (Matt 13:3–9, 23) or that sometimes only sprouts up briefly, then dies (Matt 13:5–6). Thus, we can expect it to grow in certain areas and perhaps even to die back. Nevertheless, eventually it will come back because the latent life principle and inherent productivity of seed involves its death and renewal (John 12:24; 1 Cor 15:36). Ultimately, God gives the increase (Lev 26:3–4; Deut 8:18; 28:1–2; 1 Cor 3:6–7) and provides renewal (Jer 23:3–5; Eze 37:11–14) when and where he pleases (cf. Isa 46:10; 55:9–11; Amos 9:13; Zech 4:8–9; John 3:8).

---

[14] See the function of tongues as a sign of judgment-curse on Israel, Acts 2: 4–40; 1 Cor 14:20–21. See: Kenneth L. Gentry, Jr., *Nourishment from the Word: Select Studies in Reformed Theology* (Ventura Calif.: Nordskog, 2008), ch. 4; Leland Ryken, James C. Wilhoit, Tremper Longman III, eds., *Dictionary of Biblical Imagery* (Downers Grove, Ill: InterVarsity, 1998), 876; O. Palmer Robertson, *The Final Word: A Biblical Response to the Case for Tongues and Prophecy Today* (Edinburgh: Banner of Truth, 1993), 41–50.

[15] "Postmillennialism," *Dictionary of Premillennial Theology*, 310.

This Age / The Age to Come

Another eschatological timing issue involves the New Testament concepts of "this age" and "the age to come." Christ speaks of "this age" and another "age to come" (Matt 12:32; Mark 10:30; Luke 18:30; 20:34–35). The present age is the sin-laden present in which we live. The "age to come" refers to the eternal order (Luke 18:30); it involves the resurrection and will not include marrying (Luke 20:34–35). It is truly consummate and final.

From the linear perspective of the Old Testament, ancient Israel believes that the "age to come" will be the Messianic era that will fully arrive after their current age ends. Yet in the New Testament we learn that the "age to come" begins *in principle* with the first century coming of Christ; it *overlaps* with "this age." Thus, we are not only children of "this age" (present, sin-laden, temporal history), but are also spiritually children of "the age to come" (the final, perfected, eternal age). We have our feet in both worlds. Or as Geerhardus Vos put it: "The age to come was perceived to bear in its womb another age to come."[16]

Because of this overlap principle, this "now but not yet" perspective, we *already* spiritually share in the benefits of "the age to come." This is because the two ages are linked by Christ's ruling in both, for he has a name "far above all rule and authority and power and dominion, and every name that is named, not only in this age, but also in the one to come" (Eph 1:21). Therefore, we have already "tasted the good word of God and the powers of the age to come" (Heb 6:5), despite living in "this present evil age" (Gal 1:4).

We already experience resurrection — spiritually: "we have passed out of death into life" (1 John 3:15; cp. John 5:24–25; Rom 6:4; Eph 2:6). And yet we still look forward to a physical resurrection beyond "this present time" (Rom 8:18–23). Indeed, we even now sit "with Him in heavenly places" so that "in the ages to come He might show the surpassing riches of his grace in kindness toward us in Christ Jesus" (Eph 2:6b–7). We already partake of the "new creation" (2 Cor 5:17; Gal 6:15), though the eternal new creation still awaits us (2 Pet 3:13).

We already enjoy the "new birth" into that new world (John 3:3; 1 Pet 1:1, 23), though we will experience the fulness of "the glory of the chil-

---

[16] Geerhardus Vos, *The Pauline Eschatology* (Phillipsburg, N.J.: P & R, 1930 [rep. 1991]), 37.

dren of God" only in the future (Rom 8:19, 23). We already possess the Spirit, who is the one who in that future age will "give life to your mortal bodies" (Rom 8:11). We already have victory over Satan (Matt 12:29; Rom 16:20; Jms 4:7), though he is the "god of this age" (2 Cor 4:4). We do good works now so that we might store up treasure "for the future" (1 Tim 6:17–19; cp. Rom 2:5–7).

The central principle uniting "this age" and "the age to come" is the resurrection. Richard Gaffin well states: "The unity of the resurrection of Christ and the resurrection of believers is such that the latter consists of two episodes in the experience of the individual believer — one which is already past, already realized, and one which is future, yet to be realized," so that our "resurrection is both already and not yet."[17]

As born again believers, two worlds co-exist in us through the Holy Spirit.[18] Thus, the "last days" (in which we live since Christ came in the first century) are unique in that they involve a merger of "this age" and the "age to come" as an "already / not yet" phenomenon. Truly, "Christ's life, and especially death and resurrection through the Spirit, launched the end-time new creation for God's glory."[19]

Christ's "Imminent" Return

A prominent feature of prophetic interest in our current evangelical setting is the widespread conviction among Bible-believers is that we are living in the very last days just before Christ's return. That is, that we are living "in the shadow of the second coming,"[20] that we are in a "countdown to Armageddon."[21] We often find linked with a radical misunderstanding of the last days the doctrine of the *imminent return of Christ*, es-

---

[17] Richard B. Gaffin, Jr., *Resurrection and Redemption: A Study in Paul's Soteriology* (2d ed: Phillipsburg, NJ: Presbyterian and Reformed, 1978), 60.

[18] Vos, *Pauline Eschatology*, 38.

[19] Beale in Kent E. Brpwer and Mark W. Elliott, eds. *Eschatology in Bible & Theology: Evangelical Essays at the Dawn of a New Millennium* (Downers Grove, Ill.: InterVarsity, 1997), 23.

[20] Timothy P. Weber, *Living in the Shadow of the Second Coming: American Premillennialism 1875-1982* (Grand Rapids, Mich.: Zondervan/Academie), 1983.

[21] Hal Lindsey, *The 1980s: Countdown to Armageddon* (New York: Bantam, 1980).

pecially among dispensationalists and premillennialists — but also even with amillennialists.[22]

The imminent coming itself

John F. Walvoord explains imminency for us: "The hope of the return of Christ to take the saints to heaven is presented in John 14 as an imminent hope. There is no teaching of any intervening event. The prospect of being taken to heaven at the coming of Christ is not qualified by description of any signs or prerequisite events."[23] Gerald Stanton states that imminency means the Lord's return "is next on the program and may take place at any time."[24] Indeed, "his coming is next on the revealed program of God."[25] It is "the next predicted event in God's prophetic timetable."[26]

Unfortunately, Walvoord's statement clashes with the wider body of his work. In a later work, *Prophecy in the New Millennium*, he dogmatically asserts: "In the centuries of human progress since Adam, the twentieth century deserves its own unique place as an era of unusual prophetic fulfillment that is unequaled in history, except possibly in the first century."[27] Which is it: (1) The Bible offers "no teaching of any intervening event"? Or (2) the twentieth century is "an era of unusual prophetic fulfillment"? If prophecies are fulfilled in the twentieth century are they not "intervening" events that must occur before the second coming?

In another work, Walvoord even provides a detailed list of the "predicted order of prophetic events related to Israel," which include the German holocaust, the United Nations action to form Israel as a nation

---

[22] See premillennialist J. B. Payne's *Imminent Appearing of Christ* (Grand Rapids: Eerdmans, 1962). Even amillennialists can sound like dispensationalists when they cry the alarm: "The year 1990 and the decade it initiates will bring that tribulation ever closer." Hanko, "The Illusory Hope of the Rapture," *Standard Bearer* 66:7 (Jan. 1, 1990) 155.

[23] John F. Walvoord, *The Rapture Question* (Grand Rapids: Zondervan, 1957), 78–79.

[24] Gerald B. Stanton in Thomas D. Ice and Timothy Demy, eds., *When the Trumpet Sounds* (Eugene, Ore.: Harvest, 1995), 222.

[25] Stanton *When the Trumpet Sounds*, 233.

[26] Wayne A. Brindle, "Imminence," *Popular Encylopedia*, 144.

[27] John F. Walvoord, *Prophecy in the New Millennium: Fresh Look at Future Events* (Grand Rapids: Kregel, 2001), 11.

— and more.[28] He sets these out in a table and states that they occur in this "predicted order." In fact, "in the predictions that Christ made almost 2,000 years ago, He accurately portrayed the progress in the present age" so that "all these situations have been fulfilled in history."[29] LaHaye agrees: "there are more fulfilled signs today than in any previous age."[30]

Furthermore, many dispensationalist writers hold this imminency doctrine quite inconsistently. For they simultaneously hold that Revelation 2 and 3 outline the entire church Age up into our own era.[31]

For instance, Towns outlines the "history" forecast in the letters, showing that Philadelphia points to 1750–1900, while Laodicea deals with the time from 1900 to the present.[32] (Though he apparently has changed his view in his article in the *Dictionary of Premillennial Theology*. He now argues that the Philadelphia era lasts a full ten years more, ending in 1910.[33]) The *Popular Encyclopedia of Bible Prophecy* holds that the Philadelphia period starts exactly twenty years earlier: "Philadelphia — Missionary church (AD 1730–1900)."[34]

But now we must ask: How could Christ's return be *imminent* in the first century if Scripture prophesies events unfolding up through history even to our day? Would these prophecies have failed if Christ returned (imminently) in the second century?

The date-setting problem

Often dispensationalists try to distinguish between Christ's return being *imminent* and its being *soon*. This is a defensive maneuver to protect

---

[28] John F. Walvoord, *Prophecy Knowledge Handbook* (Grand Rapids: Zondervan, 1990), 382.

[29] *Prophecy Knowledge Handbook*, 383.

[30] LaHaye in Ice and Demy, *When the Trumpet Sounds*, 429.

[31] John F. Walvoord, *The Revelation of Jesus Christ* (Chicago: Moody, 1966), 52; Pentecost, *Things to Come*, 149; Charles Caldwell Ryrie, *Revelation* (Chicago: Moody, 1968), 24ff; *Scofield Reference Bible,* 1331–2; *NSRB*, 1353.

[32] Elmer Towns in *Prophecy Study Bible*, 1495.

[33] Elmer Towns, "Present Age, the Course of this," *Dictionary of Premillennial Theology,* 313–14.

[34] *Popular Encyclopedia of Biblical Prophecy*, 353. Oddly the seven church periods generally start on exact dates opening a new decade (excluding Smyrna and Sardis), whereas the dispensations widely vary in start and stop points (except for the last dispensation which is exactly 1000 years).

them against charges of date-setting. This attempt fails, however, because it is inconsistently held. In a letter to me dated June 1, 1994, from Thomas D. Ice, Executive Director of the Pre-Trib Research Center, Ice writes: "We distinguish between imminent and soon in the sense that soon would require a near coming, while imminent would allow, but not require a soon coming."[35] Bundled in that very letter was his first newsletter entitled: "The Pre-Trib Research Center: A New Beginning."[36] The first sentence of the newsletter (once past the headings) was: "Our purpose is to awaken in the Body of Christ a new awareness of the soon coming of Jesus." The system giveth and taketh away. In fact, in a book edited by Ice, Tim LaHaye speaks of "the soon coming of Christ."[37]

Ironically, dispensationalists should be the last people to seek signs of the approaching end, for such a quest undermines their most distinctive doctrine: the ever-imminent, signless, secret rapture.[38] Yet, date-setting has long plagued premillennialism, especially dispensationalism.[39] The last quarter-century is particularly rife with cries of the approaching end.

---

[35] See also: Walvoord, *Prophecy in the New Millennium*, 128. Wayne A. Brindle, "Imminence," *Popular Encyclopedia*, 144.

[36] Tim LaHaye, "The Pre-Trib Research Center: A New Beginning," in *Pre-Trib Perspectives,* 1:1 (May, 1994): 1.

[37] LaHaye in Ice and Demy, *When the Trumpet Sounds*, 429.

[38] Though some complain that the idea of a "secret" rapture was created as a strawman term by anti-dispensationalists, Hal Lindsey speaks of the *secret* rapture in his *Late Great Planet Earth* (Grand Rapids: Zondervan, 1970), 142–43: "in the Rapture, only the Christians see Him — it's a mystery, a secret. When the living believers are taken out, the world is going to be mystified."

[39] See the classic historical study on the problem: Wilson, *Armageddon Now!* (1991). See also: Gumerlock, *The Day and the Hour* (2000). For an exegetical study of the error, see: DeMar, *Last Days Madness* (1999). The problem is indicated in the following popular dispensational titles: Lindsey, *Planet Earth — 2000* (1994). Sumrall, *I Predict 2000* (1987). Lewis, *Prophecy 2000: Rushing to Armageddon* (1990). Terrell, *The 90's: Decade of the Apocalypse* (1992). Hunt, *How Close Are We?: Compelling Evidence for the Soon Return of Christ* (1993). Graham, *Storm Warning* (1992). Ryrie, *The Final Countdown* (1991). Jeffries, *Armageddon: Appointment with Destiny* (1988). McKeever, *The Rapture Book: Victory in the End Times* (1987). McAlvanny, et al., *Earth's Final Days* (1994). Marrs, et al., *Storming Toward Armageddon: Essays in Apocalypse* (1992). Liardon, *Final Approach: The Opportunity and Adventure of End-Times Living* (1993). Webber and Hutchins, *Is This the Last Century?* (1979).

In 1990–91 needless American fears over the thirty day First Gulf War fuel the flames of date-setting, much like World War I did seventy-five years earlier.[40] During that war Hal Lindsey wrote: "At the time of this writing, virtually the entire world may be plunged into a war in which this city [Babylon] may emerge with a role and destiny that few have any inkling of." Later he sums up: "This is the most exciting time to be alive in all of human history. We are about to witness the climax of God's dealing with man."[41] LaHaye's chapter in *When the Trumpet Sounds* (1995) is titled "Twelve Reasons Why This Could Be the Terminal Generation."[42]

Even noted dispensational theologians engage in date-setting. Ironically, in the summer of 1990, as the Gulf War clouds loomed, Walvoord's book review appeared in which he wrote disparagingly of my insistence that dispensationalists are date-setters: "So premillennialism and dispensationalism have been derided as a date-setting system of doctrine, even though very few of its adherents indulge in this procedure."[43] But in 2001 Walvoord writes: "Many indications exist that human history is reaching its climax in end-time events."[44]

The New Testament teaches, however, that the Lord's glorious, bodily return will be in its *distant* and *unknowable* future. It is neither *imminent* nor *datable*. Bahnsen notes that "distinctive to [postmillennialism] is the

---

[40] Arthur Pink wrote: "Brethren, the end of the Age is upon us. All over the world, reflecting minds are discerning the fact that we are on the very eve of another of those far-reaching crises which make the history of our race.... Those who look out on present conditions are forced to conclude that the consummation of the dispensation is at hand.... The sands in the hour glass of this Day of Salvation have almost run out. The signs of the Times demonstrate it.... The Signs are so plain they cannot be mis-read, though the foolish may close their eyes and refuse to examine them." Arthur W. Pink, *The Redeemer's Return* (Ashland, Kent.: Calvary Baptist Church, rep. [1918]), 318–19.

[41] Hal Lindsey, *The Rise of Babylon and the Persian Gulf Crisis* (Palos Verdes, Calif.: Lindsey Ministries, 1991), 2, 51. See also: Betty Lynn, "The Gulf War and the Coming Fall of Babylon," *Christian World Report*, 3:2 (Feb. 1991): 1.

[42] LaHaye in Ice and Demy, *When the Trumpet Sounds*, ch. 21.

[43] John F. Walvoord, "Review of House Divided," *Bibliotheca Sacra* 147 (July/Sept. 1990): 372.

[44] John F. Walvoord, *Prophecy in the New Millennium: Fresh Look at Future Events*. Grand Rapids (Kregel, 2001), 26.

denial of the imminent physical return" of Christ.[45] Mathison agrees: "Scripture simply does not teach the dispensational doctrine of the 'imminent' return of Christ."[46] Let us see how this is so.

Christ denies imminency

As we have seen in our study, Jesus speaks frequently on the kingdom, by parable and by direct discourse. And in several of his parables on the kingdom and kingdom service, he specifically denies an imminent return. The long-term perspective is also implied in other texts in the New Testament.

Kingdom parables. Jesus' Parable of the Ten Virgins elaborates on "the kingdom of heaven" (Matt 25:1). But in that parable he warns that "while the bridegroom was *delayed*, they [the virgins] all slumbered and slept" (Matt 25:5). This delay language does not expect an *any-moment* return, but a return after a long while. In fact, the very point of this parable is that the "wise" virgins prepare for his *delayed* return. But the foolish ones expect him soon and do not prepare themselves for the long run (Matt 25:2–3, 8).

In an associated parable he teaches that "the kingdom of heaven is like a man traveling to a *far* country, who called his own servants and delivered his goods to them." The imagery here presents the man traveling to a far country (heaven!) so that "after a *long* time the lord of those servants came and settled accounts with them" (Matt 25:14, 19). Here we find no allusion to an any-moment return. Indeed, once again we find just the opposite.

The great commission. Matthew 28:20 states that the Great Commission will stretch through "all the days" (literal translation of the Greek, *pasas tas hēmeras*). This indicates a great many days must transpire before the end comes. We should expect this since the parables of the mustard seed and leaven set forth a *gradually* developing kingdom, which must continue to grow until it *finally* dominates the world's landscape and penetrates all of the world's cultures. This surely suggests a long period of time.

---

[45] Greg L. Bahnsen, "The *Prima Facie* Acceptability of Postmillennialism," *Journal of Christian Reconstruction*, 3:2 (Winter 1976–77): 60. Cf. O. T. Allis, *Prophecy and the Church* (Philadelphia: Presbyterian and Reformed, 1945), 173–174.

[46] Keith A. Mathison, *Postmillennialism: An Eschatology of Hope* (Phillipsburg, N.J.: Presbyterian and Reformed, 1999), 206.

Despite Jesus being the best teacher to ever walk the earth, his disciples were often-confused at his teaching (Matt 16:21–23; Luke 24:25; John 20:9), apparently due to their having imbibed the erroneous teaching of the first-century Pharisees. We see their confusion regarding the timing of his kingdom just before his ascension: "They asked Him, saying, 'Lord, will You at *this time* restore the kingdom to Israel?' And He said to them, 'It is not for you to know *times* [*chronos*] or seasons which the Father has put in His own authority" (Acts 1:7).

The Lord's answer to this timing question in Acts 1:7 shows that he anticipates a long period before the end. The Greek word for "times" in his answer is *chronos*, which indicates a long period of uncertain duration. In fact, it appears in the plural, which suggests "a rather long period of time composed of several shorter ones."[47] As premillennialists Blomberg and Chung put it: this "Acts passage utilizes the two broadest words in Hellenistic Greek for 'time' (*chronos* and *kairos*)," which precludes any "claim to be able to pin down end-times events to any definable period of time."[48]

Peter denies imminency

Peter seems to reflect this long-term waiting in Acts 3:19, where he speaks of the "*times* of refreshing." After all, here "the plural may be intended to convey the idea that it is a long way off" (cf. 2 Tim 3:1).[49] Interestingly, "the only errors mentioned in the New Testament respecting the time of our Lord's coming, all consist in dating it too early."[50] We see this problem in the passages cited above, as well as in the famous passages: 2 Thessalonians 2:1–3 and 2 Peter 3:3–4.

In the 2 Peter 3 passage Peter warns Christians to expect pagans to taunt them about the delay in Christ's coming: "Know this first of all, that in the last days mockers will come with their mocking, following after their own lusts, and saying, 'Where is the promise of His coming? For

---

[47] *A Greek-English Lexicon of the New Testament and Other Early Christian Literature*, ed by F. Wilbur Gingrich and Frederick W. Danker (2d. ed.: Chicago: University of Chicago Press, 1979), 1092.

[48] Blomberg and Chung, *Historic Premillennialism*, xii.

[49] C. S. C. Williams, *A Commentary on the Acts of the Apostles* (Peabody, Mass: Hendrickson, 1964), 71.

[50] William Urwick quoted in Brown, *Christ's Second Coming*, 41n.

ever since the fathers fell asleep, all continues just as it was from the beginning of creation'" (2 Pet 3:3–4).

Peter then explains the delay while urging *patience*: "But do not let this one fact escape your notice, beloved, that with the Lord one day is like a thousand years, and a thousand years like one day. The Lord is not slow about His promise, as some count slowness, but is patient toward you, not wishing for any to perish but for all to come to repentance" (2 Pet 3:8–9). He even employs the period of thousand years in his explanation of the delay.

Conclusion

In this chapter we focused on three timing issues that are important in both correct prophetic understanding and contemporary prophecy discussion. Obviously many more issues deserve consideration, but space limitations forbid it.[51]

The issue of God's gradualistic method and a denial of imminency generally distinguish postmillennialism from the other evangelical options. The postmillennial viewpoint denies imminency altogether.

The matter of "this age / the age to come" is broadly agreed upon in all four evangelical options, but its full significance is lost in the dispensational system. And the postmillennial understanding of and commitment to this principle is often not well understood by the other eschatological systems.

Once we have a proper grasp of each of these temporal issues, the case for postmillennialism is greatly strengthened.

REVIEW QUESTIONS FOR DISCUSSION

These questions deal directly with the material in this chapter. The answers can be found in the chapter.
1. What is the principle of gradualism? How does it differ from catastrophism?
2. Explain the principle of gradualism as it is a necessary means for understanding God's actions in history, especially eschatology.

---

[51] For more detailed information on these and many other matters, see my: *He Shall Have Dominion: A Postmillennial Eschatology* (Draper, Vir.: NiceneCouncil.com, 2009).

3. What are some examples of God's employing the gradualistic principle in his own work?
4. Can you discern a possible link between Jesus' Parable of the Mustard Seed and Ezekiel's vision of the cedar twig? What are the points of contact?
5. Explain the concept of the overlap of "this age" and "the age to come." How does this impact our understanding of eschatology?
6. What does the dispensationalist mean by the doctrine of the "imminent" return of Christ? Explain his thinking and argument.
7. What are some biblical evidences that imminency is a faulty doctrine?
8. Though dispensationalists hold to the imminent return of Christ as a necessary doctrine for dispensationalism (and as an objection against postmillennialism), they breach this doctrine from time to time. Give a sample or two of how they deny their own imminency doctrine.
9. What is the date-setting problem that plagues dispensationalism? How is it contrary to Scripture?
10. Why is the proper understanding of these timing issues important for developing a proper eschatological outlook?

STRETCHING FURTHER

1. Can you think of other biblical instances of God's working gradually in history that are not listed in this chapter?
2. Can you think of some other eschatological statements that require gradualism for explaining God's kingdom work in history.
3. Dispensationalists often see the Parable of the Mustard Seed as picturing the corruption of the church in history. They do so partly on the basis of the fact that the birds mentioned here appear in the first parable as carrying off the seed that the sower intended to plant. But how else can you explain the birds finally nesting in the branches of the tree grown from a seed?
4. Can you think of any examples of date-setting in dispensational circles?
5. What were some new ideas you learned from this chapter?

Chapter 12
OBJECTIONS TO POSTMILLENNIALISM

A vigorous eschatological debate has been conducted for a very long time in evangelical circles. And it continues today. Unfortunately, postmillennialism suffers the most from misunderstanding. This partly relates to the fact that it is currently the minority viewpoint, having declined much since its heyday during the great missionary expansion of Christianity in the 1700s–1800s.

Due to ongoing nature of this problem of misunderstanding it will serve us well to answer some of the leading objections to the postmillennial viewpoint. Answering objections will not only serve a defensive purpose in removing misunderstandings, but in doing so will provide further positive affirmation of this optimistic eschatology. I will categorize the objections into three classes: practical, doctrinal, and biblical objections. Let us start with:

Practical Objections

The most popular objections against postmillennialism are the practical concerns. They are frequently brought against postmillennialism in the popular literature. But to no avail, for there are easy answers to them. Let's see how this is so.

"World conditions contradict postmillennialism"

Too many evangelicals get their understanding of the biblical prophecy from reading the newspapers through their faulty interpretive lens. They point out a truly conservative Christian concern: America is in a great moral and spiritual decline today. And such a decline contradicts postmillennialism's historical expectations. For instance, dispensationalist theologian Paul N. Benware responds against postmillennialism that "the idea that the world is getting better and better does not at all seem to be in line with reality. The evidence points rather to a world that is growing more and more wicked."[1]

---

[1] Paul N. Benware, *Understanding End Times Prophecy: A Comprehensive Guide* (Chicago: Moody, 1995), 128.

Postmillennialists are well aware of world conditions. And yet we continue with our optimistic outlook despite these contemporary conditions. Consider two postmillennial responses to this complaint.

This objection uses a wrong method. That is, this argument selects too narrow a sample from history. When we consider the broader historical scheme, this problem vanishes away. World conditions, and especially conditions for Christians, have actually improved greatly since Christianity first arose 2000 years ago.

In the first three centuries of our era, Christianity was relentlessly assaulted by the Jews on the one hand and cruelly persecuted by the Romans on the other. Thus, in light of the big picture: Are Christians better off today than they were in the first two or three centuries? Are world conditions worse today in Christian areas than they were in the first century under Nero? Anyone who is aware of the Roman persecutions against the early church should understand that believers today are in a much better situation in large portions of the earth today.

This objection assumes an erroneous definition. We must understand that nothing in the postmillennial definition requires *either* relentlessly forward progress of kingdom conditions *or* the kingdom's reaching its highest advance by any particular date. As noted in the preceding chapter, postmillennialism is gradualistic. The gradualistic postmillennialism presented in this book simply teaches that *before the end* the kingdom of God will reach world-dominating proportions.

Thus, until history ends this argument cannot undermine the postmillennial hope. Glorious revivals may yet occur — and postmillennialists are confident they will.

"Postmillennialism undermines watchfulness"

Also as noted in the last chapter, postmillennialism holds to a *long-term* view of the future. Because of this many evangelicals complain that this eschatology actually undermines a spiritual motive to serving Christ. That is, postmillennialism discourages Christians from watching for the Lord's return. By the very nature of the case postmillennialism denies the "imminent" return of Christ.

We see this line of complaint in best-selling dispensationalist author Dave Hunt's writings. Hunt laments postmillennialism because, in it "there is an increasing antagonism against eagerly watching and waiting for Christ's return, which surely was the attitude of the early church."[2] Hunt represents many others who see our denial of the imminency of Christ's return as destroying a spur to sanctification. But consider:

This objection is based on a erroneous understanding. To deny that Christ could return at any moment does not destroy a spur to holiness. Surely sanctification is not encouraged by believing a falsehood (that Christ will return in one's own lifetime). Those who argue for an "any moment" view of the return of Christ as a major spur for holy living ultimately root sanctification in erroneous expectations. After all, Christ was not to return in the first 2000 years of Christian history, as we can now see. Were early Christians who expected Jesus to return at any minute made holy by believing an error?

This objection overlooks a more likely event. Any expectation of the possible return of Christ should be a weaker spur to sanctification than the realization that we could die this very minute. We are statistically more certain that we *will* die in a relatively short time (Psa 90:4–6, 10; 1 Pet 1:24) than we are that Christ will return today. This has proven true for 2000 years. And this was the very point of his Parable of the Rich Barn Owner (Luke 12:16–20): the barn owner did not take into account the fact that he could die at any moment.

This objection forgets the ultimate reality. Because of our doctrine of God, we should know that we are living constantly under the moment-by-moment scrutiny of a righteous Judge. We cannot escape his presence during any moment of life, for "there is no creature hidden from his sight, but all things are naked and open to the eyes of Him to whom *we must give account*" (Heb 4:13). David tried to escape God's scrutiny, but failed (Psa 139:7–12). The theological *certainty* of our present openness to the Lord ought to move us to serve him more faithfully even than the *possibility* that he may return today.

"Postmillennialism is basically liberal"

Many non postmillennialists see historical optimism as a liberal, social-gospel approach to history. Thus, postmillennialism seems to tend towards liberalism. For instance, dispensationalist scholar John Walvoord argues that postmillennialism cannot resist the tendency to liberalism in

---

[2] Dave Hunt, *Whatever Happened to Heaven?* (Eugene, Ore.: Harvest, 1988), 8.

that it "lends itself to liberalism with only minor adjustments."[3] Pentecost adds that in postmillennialism there is a "trend toward liberalism, which postmillennialism could not meet, because of its spiritualizing principle of interpretation."[4] How shall we respond?

Such an objection involves an impossible definition. Actually the postmillennial response is quite easy: It is absolutely *impossible* for there to be liberal postmillennialists. How can we say this? After all, the very term "postmillennial" means that Christ will return after ("post") millennial conditions ("millennium"). Now we must ask: What liberal believes that Christ will return *ever*? By definition liberalism denies that Christ is God in the flesh; they believe he was merely a first-century rabbi who is now long dead.

Such an objection is invalid on its very surface. No evangelical theology (such as postmillennialism) can lead to liberalism with only "minor adjustments." Who would consider these as minor issues needing adjustment: postmillennialists believe in the existence of the Creator, the inspiration of Scripture, the deity of Christ, his physical resurrection from the dead, his second coming to end history, and more. Any shift from evangelical postmillennialism to liberalism requires fundamental changes, not minor adjustments. The differences separating postmillennialism and liberalism represent the enormous gulf separating supernaturalism from naturalism. The systems of thought are not at all close together.

Such an objection is interpretively naive. Dispensationalist J. Dwight Pentecost charges that postmillennialism's "spiritualizing principle of interpretation" lends itself easily to liberalism. He promotes the literalist approach and sees that as protecting the Christian from liberalism. But this sort of argument can be turned on the dispensationalist. Could we not argue that *premillennialism leads to cultism* because of the literalistic hermeneutic of such premillennial cults as Mormonism? Does not Pente-

---

[3] John F. Walvoord, *The Millennial Kingdom* (Findlay, Ohio: Dunham, 1959), 35; also 34. This is an incredible and indefensible assertion. Postmillennialists believe in the visible, glorious return of Christ to cause the physical resurrection of the dead and to hold the Great Judgment of all men, assigning some to heaven and others to hell. No liberal theologian holds any of these fundamental assertions.

[4] J. Dwight Pentecost, *Things to Come: A Study in Biblical Eschatology* (Grand Rapids: Zondervan, 1958), 386.

cost himself admit that literalism was the method applied by the Christ-rejecting Pharisees?[5]

Doctrinal Objections

We will now move to a more serious class of objections: those related to doctrinal issues. Eschatology is a doctrine, therefore, any doctrinal problems would self-destructive for the system.

"Sin undermines the postmillennial hope"

Many evangelical scholars reject postmillennialism because of the Bible's strong commitment to the doctrine of sin. According to amillennialist Hanko, postmillennialism "is a mirage, therefore, a false hope, because it fails to reckon properly with the fact of sin" and "cannot take sin as seriously as do the Scriptures."[6] This sounds like a strong objection on the surface. Its beauty, however, is only skin deep.

This complaint surprisingly overlooks the reality of salvation. We must note the obvious: despite the presence of sin in the world, sinners are nevertheless converted to Christ. Each convert to Christ was at one time a totally depraved sinner. Were you a sinner before conversion to Christ? And yet we have hundreds of millions of Christians in the world today — despite "the fact of sin."

Besides, salvation comes by the gospel which is the power of God unto salvation (Rom 1:16). Is man's sin more powerful than God's grace? How can we deny the gospel's power that has already saved millions of depraved sinners? What God can do for one sinner he can do for another.

"Christ's kingdom is a failure so far"

Amillennialist Kim Riddlebarger charges postmillennialism with this error: "Indeed, the nagging question remains, 'If postmillenarians are correct about their millennial expectations, what does this say about the progress of the kingdom thus far?' Must we speak of the history of the church to date as an abject failure, although a golden age presumably lies

---

[5] Pentecost, *Things to Come*, 17–19.
[6] Herman Hanko, "The Illusory Hope of Postmillennialism," *Standard Bearer* 66:7 (Jan. 1, 1990), 159.

ahead? Of course not. But this is the direction in which postmillennial expectations push us."[7] How shall we respond?

This objection is based on a truncated definition. Such complainants forget the postmillennial definition of the kingdom: The kingdom is *by divine design* to enter the world "mysteriously" (Matt 13:11) *growing* from a "seed" to a "mature plant," from imperceptible, fragile-appearing beginnings to obvious, world-dominating fullness. How can its early stages be a "failure" because they are unlike its final stages?

Christ's kingdom rule is no more a "failure" than a seed is a "failure" because it is not a mature tree with edible fruit. The kingdom is not failing of its purpose any more than a baby is failing because he lacks teeth, cannot walk, and cannot talk. Both the seed and the baby are *successes* when they operate *according to their design*, a design which promotes *gradually developing maturity*. Gradual kingdom growth to full dominion is God's design — and the postmillennial hope.

This objection overlooks historical reality. The postmillennialist argues that the kingdom *has grown* since the first century. We are delighted that we are no longer being thrown to the lions as a hated minority. The kingdom has not attained its full maturity, but it has definitely grown as prophesied. After all, the postmillennial definition highlights "increasing gospel success" and which "gradually" produces its effect. Progress *has* been made; the kingdom is *not* failing.

Biblical Objections

The most serious class of problems for any eschatological system is the biblical objection. If one's eschatology does not arise from Scripture itself, it is not a biblical doctrine. We must have a "thus saith the Lord" justifying our prophetic system. Let us consider some of the leading biblical texts brought against the postmillennial hope.

Matthew 7:13–14

> "Enter by the narrow gate; for wide is the gate and broad is the way that leads to destruction, and there are many who go in by it. Because narrow is the gate and difficult is the way which leads to life, and there are few who find it."

---

[7] Kim Riddlebarger, *A Case for Amillennialism: Understanding the End Times* (Grand Rapids: Baker, 2003), 238.

This famous passage seems to undermine the postmillennial hope of a world converted to Christ. How does postmillennialism account for this comment by our Lord himself?

We must discern the Lord's purpose behind this statement. Postmillennialist B. B. Warfield noted of this passage that "our Lord's purpose is rather ethical impression than prophetic disclosure."[8] That is, Jesus is urging his disciples to consider their *present situation* in which they live. They must look around and see that many are dying without salvation and too few are being saved.

Jesus is not prophesying the future. He is pressing his disciples to engage the present. He is aksing: What will they do about the current, sad situation? Do they love him enough to seek to reverse it? Christ's challenge to them is ethical. This is much like his statement in John 4:35, where he is prompting his disciples to evangelistic endeavor: "Do you not say, 'There are still four months and then comes the harvest'? Behold, I say to you, lift up your eyes and look at the fields, for they are already white for harvest!"

We must recognize the relative nature of his comments. Interestingly, just a few verses later and very soon after stating these words, the Lord declares: "I say to you that many [*polus*, the same word in Matt 7:13 for the lost] will come from east and west, and sit down with Abraham, Isaac, and Jacob in the kingdom of heaven" (Matt 8:11).

In other places the Bible speaks of the vast number of the redeemed. For instance, Revelation 7:9: "After these things I looked, and behold, a great multitude which no one could number, of all nations, tribes, peoples, and tongues, standing before the throne and before the Lamb, clothed with white robes, with palm branches in their hands." And of course we should recall those prophecies which speak of "all nations" flowing into the kingdom (e.g., Isa 2:2–4; Mic 4:1–4).

Matthew 13:36–39

"Then Jesus sent the multitude away and went into the house. And His disciples came to Him, saying, 'explain to us the parable of the tares of the field.' He answered and said to them: 'He who sows the good seed is the Son of Man. The field is the world, the good seeds are the sons of the kingdom, but the tares are the

---

[8] Benjamin B. Warfield, "Are There Few That Be Saved?," in Warfield, *Biblical and Theological Studies* (Philadelphia: Presbyterian and Reformed, rep. 1952), 338.

sons of the wicked one. The enemy who sowed them is the devil, the harvest is the end of the age, and the reapers are the angels.'"

In his treatment of these words of Christ, dispensationalist Walvoord states that "the parable does not support the postmillennial idea that the Gospel will be triumphant and bring in a golden age."[9] He sees this as evidence that the church's growth will be matched by the growth of Satan's kingdom, thus discounting the postmillennial hope of Christian dominance.

The basic definitional problem. Frequently, non-postmillennialists seem to imply that postmillennialism expects an "each-and-every" *salvific universalism*. With that false perception critics press this passage as evidence that Christianity will never gain the upper hand in the world. But postmillennialism teaches that despite the enormous worldwide success of the gospel, we will always have a mixture of the unrighteous and the righteous. Gospel success will never totally root out either sin or sinners from history. This remains true even during the kingdom's highest development in the future. We never expect global universalism to prevail before Christ's return.

The basic interpretive problem. This parable portrays the entire world as God's field, where he desires to plant wheat: he "sowed good seed in his field" (Matt 13:24) and "the field is the world" (Matt 13:38). God expends the effort in order to create a field of wheat (the righteous, Matt 13:38a) in all the world. An enemy (the devil, Matt 13:39) intervenes and sows tares (the wicked, Matt 13:38b). Surely Satan does not sow the tares with equal success! We should doubt this prospect altogether due to the nearby Parables of the Mustard Seed and Leaven (Matt 13:31–33).

Actually, the point of the Parable of the Tares is that tares will be found among the predominant wheat: the tares are the intruders, not the wheat. The Son of Man returns to a *wheat* field, not a tare field. The tares must be left alone *for the sake of the wheat*.

Luke 18:8

"I tell you that He will avenge them speedily. Nevertheless, when the Son of Man comes, will He really find faith on the earth?"

---

[9] John F. Walvoord, *Prophecy Knowledge Handbook* (Wheaton, Ill.: Victor, 1990), 373.

Regarding this verse dispensationalists Wayne House and Thomas Ice argue that: "This is 'an inferential question to which a negative answer is expected.' So this passage is saying that at the second coming Christ will not find, literally, 'the faith' upon the earth."[10] Were this the case, postmillennialism would certainly be mistaken. How could Christians be optimistic if the entire Christian faith is prophetically determined to disappear from the earth? Unfortunately for the pessimistic readings of this passage, this is not the case as we may see from the following observations:

This objection misses Christ's point. This passage is not dealing with Christianity's future existence at all. In the context, the Lord is dealing with the matter of *fervent prayer*. In the Greek "faith" has a definite article before it. As a result it refers to *the* faith already mentioned: the faith of the praying widow in Christ's parable: "Then He spoke a parable to them, that men always ought to pray and not lose heart" (Luke 18:1). Christ's teaching is not dealing with the question as to whether or not Christianity will exist in the future. Rather it is focusing on the question: Will Christians still be persevering in prayer? But there is more.

This objection misconstrues Christ's grammar. We must note that, contrary to House and Ice, the form of Christ's question does *not* expect a "negative answer." The Funk-Blass-Debrunner Greek grammar notes that the implied answer to the question is "ambiguous,"[11] because the Greek word used here (*ara*) implies only "a tone of suspense or impatience in interrogation."[12]

This objection misunderstands Christ's goal. The Lord appears to be focusing on his imminent coming in *judgment upon Israel*, not his distant second advent at the end of history. Jesus clearly speaks of a *soon-coming* vindication of his people: "I tell you that He will avenge them *speedily*" (Luke 18:8a; cp. Rev 1:1; 6:9–10). He is urging his disciples to endure in prayer through the troublesome times coming upon them. In fact, the

---

[10] H. Wayne House and Thomas D. Ice, *Dominion Theology: Blessing or Curse?* (Portland, Ore.: Multnomah, 1988), 229.

[11] F. Blass and A. DeBrunner. *A Greek Grammar of the New Testament and Other Early Christian Literature*, trans. and Ed. by Robert W. Funk (Chicago: University of Chicago Press, 1961), 226.

[12] Walter Baur, W. F. Arndt, F. W. Gingrich, and Frederick William Danker, *A Greek-English Lexicon of the New Testament and other Early Christian* Literature (3d. ed.: Chicago: University Press, 2000), 127.

preceding context of Luke 18 speaks of Jerusalem's approaching destruction (Luke 17:22–37).

This objection overlooks Christ's implication. In the final analysis, no evangelical millennial view supposes that absolutely *no* faith will exist on the earth at the Lord's return. Yet, to read the postmillennial objectors, Luke 18:8 supposedly teaches that Christianity will be totally and absolutely dead at his return.

2 Timothy 3:1–4, 13

"Realize this, that in the last days difficult times will come. For men will be lovers of self, lovers of money, boastful, arrogant, revilers, disobedient to parents, ungrateful, unholy, unloving, irreconcilable, malicious gossips, without self-control, brutal, haters of good, treacherous, reckless, conceited, lovers of pleasure rather than lovers of God. . . . But evil men and impostors will proceed from bad to worse, deceiving and being deceived."

A quick reading of Paul's last epistle seems to undermine the postmillennial hope. Amillennialist Herman Hoekema references this passage and declares: "the postmillennial expectation of a future golden age before Christ's return does not do justice to the continuing tension in the history of the world between the kingdom of God and the forces of evil."[13] How may the postmillennialist respond to this powerful objection?

This objection forgets Paul's historical context. As with most of his epistles, Paul's letter is an occasional epistle. That is, it is dealing with a particular historical occasion in the first century. He is speaking of things that his associate Timothy (2 Tim 1:2) will be facing and enduring (2 Tim 3:10–14). He is not prophesying about the all future expectations for the faith. The letter is addressed to Timothy (2 Tim 1:1–6) about circumstances he and Paul are facing (cf. 2 Tim 1:13–15; 4:1), which will require spiritual strength on Timothy's part (2 Tim 2:1–2, 7, 14; 4:5).

This objection misunderstands meaning of "the last days." In the New Testament the "last days" cover the entire period from the first coming of Christ until his second coming. We see this in several places. Peter's Pentecostal sermon clearly applies the "last days" concept to the first century when he explains the outburst of tongues-speaking: "This is what was spoken of through the prophet Joel: In the last days...." (Acts

---

[13] Anthony A. Hoekema, *The Bible and the Future* (Grand Rapids: Eerdmans, 1979), 180.

2:16–17a; see discussion of Isa 2 in ch 3 above). Thus, this is not declaring what the final future, the very last day of earth will be like. This is important when we note that:

This objection misinterprets the text itself. The text does not demand constant bad times lie in the future. Paul is stating that difficult "times" (*kairoi*) will come during the last days (the period between the first and second advents). The Greek term Paul employs here is a plural, *kairoi*, which indicates "seasons." It is erroneous to read this reference to *some* "seasons" of difficulty as if it said *all* seasons will be difficult. Postmillennial gradualism expects that "seasons" of perilous times will punctuate history. We do not believe that Paul is saying that this is all that we can expect in history.

This objection misapplies Paul's concern. This passage does expect an accelerating moral collapse as history unfolds. Citing 2 Timothy 3:13 in the debate leaves the unwarranted impression that things shall irrevocably become worse and worse in history. But the verse actually says: "evil men and impostors will proceed from bad to worse, deceiving and being deceived." Paul is speaking of *specific evil men* becoming ethically worse, not more and more evil men becoming increasingly dominant. He is speaking of their *progressive personal degeneration*, i.e., the progressive anti-sanctification of particular evil men. He says absolutely nothing about an increase in the *number* and *power* of such evil men.

This objection overlooks Paul's optimism. Paul balances his warning about evil men with an encouraging note of optimism. As a good postmillennialist, Paul comforts Timothy by stating that these evil men "will not make further progress; for their folly will be obvious to all" (2 Tim 3:9). Since God places limits on those evil-doers, Paul speaks as a man who expects victory. How different from the modern church's widespread, pessimistic conception of the progressive, limitless power of evil in our day. Paul's conceives of the ultimate, long term impotence of evil in history.[14]

Conclusion

We have surveyed the leading objections to postmillennialism. We have looked at practical doctrinal, and biblical objections. We noted that

---

[14] Kenneth L. Gentry, Jr., *The Greatness of the Great Commission: The Christian Enterprise in a Fallen World* (Tyler, Tex.: Institute for Christian Economics, 1993), ch. 12: "Pessimism and the Great Commission."

some verses do seem to contradict the optimistic outlook of postmillennialism. But when we looked more carefully at these passages, we saw that they present no difficulty to postmillennialism.

Postmillennialism is built up from Scripture. And because of the Scripture's integrity, it does not contradict itself. The postmillennialist gladly compares Scripture with Scripture to see whether these things are so (Acts 17:11).

REVIEW QUESTIONS FOR DISCUSSION

These questions deal directly with the material in this chapter. The answers can be found in the chapter.

1. What are the three classes of objections brought against postmillennialism? Which do you believe to be the most significant?
2. Since postmillennialism expects an enormous improvement in world conditions, the current world situation is often brought out as proof of the failure of postmillennialism. How would you respond to this objection?
3. Since postmillennialism expects a long period of time to transpire before Christ's return, the biblical call to watchfulness is often brought out as proof of the error of postmillennialism. How would you respond to this objection?
4. If the whole race of men is fallen into sin and totally depraved, how can postmillennialists expect a worldwide improvement of world conditions?
5. Since Jesus teaches that the gate to destruction is broad and many go into it, how can postmillennialists expect that the great majority of men in the future will be Christians?
6. Since Jesus' Parable of the Tares specifically teaches that tares are left among the wheat until the end, how can postmillennialists expect a world dominated by Christianity?
7. Does postmillennialism contradict Jesus' warning that "the faith" may not exist on the earth at his return? How do we respond to this claim brought against postmillennialism?
8. How can postmillennialists account for the fact that Paul teaches that in the last days difficult times will come and men will be boastful and arrogant? This seems to be an overt denial of the postmillennial hope.

9. What is the proper interpretation of "the last days," and how is this helpful for a postmillennial understanding of Paul's warning regarding the last days?
10. You have been such a good class, that we will let you out early today. You do not have to provide a discussion of a tenth point! Ha!

STRETCHING FURTHER

1. Can you think of other objections to the postmillennial hope that are not presented in this book? (Remember: earlier chapters dealt with objections that might arise from Jesus' great tribulation teaching and John's prophecy of judgment in Revelation.)
2. Have you ever engaged a discussion of postmillennialism with a non-postmillennial friend? What was their response? Were they intrigued by the prospects? Or did they quickly dismiss it outright?
3. Have you ever read a book (other than this one) that promotes the postmillennial viewpoint? Was it compelling? Or a disappointment?
4. Have you ever read a book that spends some time criticizing the postmillennial view? Was the book balanced and careful? Or more emotional and dismissive?
5. What were some new ideas you learned from this chapter?

CONCLUSION

We have completed our study of the hope-filled eschatology called "postmillennialism." Postmillennialism teaches that the future prospects for the church and the world are glorious. We hold that a time is coming in history, continuous with the present and resulting from currently-operating, God-ordained spiritual forces, in which the overwhelming majority of men and nations will voluntarily bow in salvation to the lordship of Jesus Christ. This humble submission to his gracious scepter will issue forth in widespread righteousness, peace, and prosperity. Scripture's eschatology is victory-oriented. In fact, as we have seen this is the message of both the Old and New Testaments.

Contrary to the superficial treatment of biblical eschatology prophecy that is so rampant in our day, we must understand the depth and majesty of Scripture's eschatological outlook. Thus, we should not expect any single text or larger passage to present an entire eschatological system. Eschatology is woven into the whole fabric of Scripture as the driving story within; it is the whole story of Scripture, not its conclusion. Properly comprehending God's eschatological message requires a working knowledge of the whole drift and framework of God's revelation in Scripture.

Postmillennialism in the Old Testament

Scripture opens with the creation account, which teaches that man, the world, and the universe were created by God, not by random, impersonal, evolutionary forces. Within this opening narrative we discover God's purpose for history. He creates man in his own image (Gen 1:26) as a material-spiritual being (Gen 2:7) and places man in the world to bring honor and glory to his Creator. He is called to exercise godly dominion throughout the world (Gen 1:26–30), beginning in Eden (Gen 2:15).

Consequently, the Christian should be predisposed to the historical victory postmillennialism expects. The Lord creates man and history for his glory; therefore, man and history *will* bring glory to him. Two powerful declarations in the New Testament emphasize this truth:

"For of Him and through Him and to Him are all things, to whom be glory forever. Amen." (Rom 11:36)

"You are worthy, O Lord, to receive glory and honor and power; for You created all things, and by Your will they exist and were created." (Rev 4:11)

This optimistic prospect becomes evident in God's response to man's fall into sin. The first promise of the gospel immediately after Adam's fall promises that the seed of the woman will crush the head of the serpent (Gen 3:15). This hope weaves its golden cord throughout Scripture all the way through to Revelation 22.

The biblical record certainly expects struggle in history due to man's fall, as we see in Genesis 3:15. But it is a struggle that leads to victory, rather than to deadlock, defeat, or despair. The Seed of the Woman (Christ) will conquer the Seed of the Serpent (Satan) — in time and on earth. This is a recurring truth in the biblical record; it defines biblical eschatology.

We may trace the victory theme through the outworking of the God's sovereign covenant. His administration of universal affairs is covenantal, unfolding in Scripture through a series of unified, successive, and judicially-related covenants. Hence, Paul speaks of "the covenants [plural] of the promise [singular]" (Eph 2:12).

The core redemptive covenant that impacts all of later Scripture is God's covenant with Abraham. In the Abrahamic Covenant God promises the spread of salvation to "all the families of the earth" (Gen 12:1–3). It is mentioned frequently in the New Testament. Paul even declares of it: "The promise to Abraham or to his descendants that he would be *heir of the world* was not through the Law, but through the righteousness of faith" (Rom 4:13). And he expressly states that all believers in Christ — whether Jews or Gentile — are the seed of Abraham: "if you belong to Christ, then you are Abraham's offspring, heirs according to promise" (Gal 3:29; cp. Rom 4:12, 16; Gal 3:6–9, 14).

After God's covenant with Abraham is established and Israel enters her Promised Land, we discover that the later Old Testament revelation continues the victory theme. The Psalms are particularly filled with eschatological hope. For instance, Psalm 2, a key Psalm alluded to frequently in the New Testament, has God promising the Messiah: "Ask of me, and I will surely give the nations as Your inheritance, / And the very ends of the earth as Your possession" (Psa 2:8).

Psalm 22:27 anticipates a time when "all the ends of the earth will remember and turn to the Lord, and all the families of the nations will worship before Thee." Psalm 66:4 reflects this hope, promising that "all the earth will worship Thee, / And will sing praises to Thee; / They will sing praises to Thy name." Psalm 72:8 utters this hope: "May he also rule from sea to sea, / And from the River to the ends of the earth."

Then as we move on to the writing prophets we find the same hope-filled anticipation. Perhaps one of the clearest prophecies appears in Isaiah 2:2–3: "In the last days, / The mountain of the house of the Lord / Will be established as the chief of the mountains, / And will be raised above the hills; / And all the nations will stream to it." This will ultimately lead nations hammering "their swords into plowshare, and their spears into pruning hooks" so that "nation will not lift up sword against nation" (Isa 2:4). But, of course, there are many more such prophecies.

Truly God's Old Testament creation, covenant, and revelation expects victory for God's people in history. But now let us consider:

Postmillennialism in the New Testament

Immediately upon entering the New Testament record, we learn of the Messiah's coming into history. He is "the Son of David, the Son of Abraham" (Matt 1:1) around whose birth we hear echoes of Old Testament victory theme, showing that his first coming begins the fruition of the promises to the fathers (Luke 1:46–55, 68–79).

Upon his entering into his public ministry, Christ immediately begins declaring that his kingdom is near. And he preaches thus because the prophesied "time is fulfilled" for it to come (Mark 1:14–15; Matt 3:2). During his ministry which is to crush Satan, we read of his power over demons presented as evidence that his kingdom has actually come (Matt 12:28). It does not lay off in the distant future, it does not await his second advent (Luke 17:20–21). After all, he claims to be king while on earth in the first century (John 12:12–15; 18:36–37).

The Lord's resurrection from the dead actually becomes the starting point for his formal kingly rule (Matt 28:18–20; Acts 2:30–31; Rom 1:3–4). And he explains that his kingdom is essentially spiritual in nature (John 18:36–37; Rom 14:17) and operates from within the heart (Luke 17: 20–21). We enter his kingdom through salvation (Col 1:12, 13; John 3:3). He rules his kingdom by his spiritual presence from heaven (John 18:36; Eph 4:8–14) and through the indwelling of the Holy Spirit (John 7:39; Rom 8:9; 1 Cor 3:16).

The New Testament promises that Christ will bring the world as a system to salvation (John 1:29; 3:17; 1 John 2:2) as the vast majority of the world's population converts to him (John 12:31; 1 Tim 2:6). The stumbling of the Jews in rejecting Christ appears to be a disappointing reversal of God's redemptive program. But their rejecting him opens up the prospect of mass conversions from among the Gentiles (Rom 11:12). Eventually the vast majority of Jews and Gentiles alike will convert, leading to the "reconciliation of the world" (Rom 11:15, 25; cp. 2 Cor 5:19).

Paul's great eschatological chapter presents Christ as currently ruling and reigning from heaven (1 Cor 15:25a). He notes that the Lord will not return in his second advent until "the end" of history (1 Cor 15:24). At that time he ends his mediatorial reign and turns the kingdom over to the Father (1 Cor 15:28). Most significantly for the postmillennial hope, Paul states that Christ's second advent will not occur until after he conquers his earthly enemies (1 Cor 15:24). He will conquer his last enemy, death, at his return when we arise from the dead (1 Cor 15:26).

Conclusion

In accordance with God's plan Christianity will overwhelm the world so that "the earth shall be full of the knowledge of the Lord as the waters cover the sea" (Isa 11:9). A day is coming when the large majority of the human race will bow before the Lord in humble worship, offering up the labor of their hands and the glory of their kingdoms to him who is "the King of kings and Lord of lords" (Rev 17:14; 19:16).

Scripture's glorious message — in *both* the Old and New Testaments — is that "every knee shall bow to Me, and every tongue shall confess to God" (Rom 14:11; cp. Isa 45:23; Phil 2:10). This is the postmillennial hope.

FOR FURTHER STUDY

Bahnsen, Greg L. *Victory in Jesus: The Bright Hope of Postmillennialism.* Texarkana, Ark.: CMP, 1999.

Bock, Darrell L., ed., *Three Views on the Millennium and Beyond.* Grand Rapids: Zondervan, 1999.

Chilton, David. *Paradise Restored: A Biblical Theology of Dominion.* Ft. Worth, Tex.: Dominion Press, 1985.

Davis, John Jefferson., *Christ's Victorious Reign: Postmillennialism Reconsidered.* Grand Rapids: Baker, 1986.

Gentry, Kenneth L., Jr. *The Greatness of the Great Commission: The Christian Enterprise in a Fallen World* . 2d. ed.: Chesnee, S.C.: Victorious Hope, 2013 (rep. 1993).

Gentry, Kenneth L., Jr. *He Shall Have Dominion: A Postmillennial Eschatology.* 2d. ed.: Chesnee, S.C.: Victorious Hope, 2009.

Kik, J. Marcellus. *An Eschatology of Victory.* Phillipsburg, N. J.: Presbyterian and Reformed, 1975.

Mathison, Keith A. *Postmillennialism: An Eschatology of Hope* (Phillipsburg, N.J.: Presbyterian and Reformed, 1999).

North, Gary. *Millennialism and Social Theory.* Tyler, Tex.: Institute for Christian Economics, 1990.

Sproul, R. C. *The Last Days according to Jesus: When Did Jesus Say He Would Return?* Grand Rapids: Baker, 2015.

www.ingramcontent.com/pod-product-compliance
Lightning Source LLC
Chambersburg PA
CBHW061759110426
42742CB00012BB/2142